CW00688691

ISBN: 9781313994774

Published by:
HardPress Publishing
8345 NW 66TH ST #2561
MIAMI FL 33166-2626

Email: info@hardpress.net
Web: http://www.hardpress.net

Of this Edition of The Percy Folio of Old English Ballads
and Romances 320 Copies have been printed on Hand-made
paper and 5 on Real Vellum. The Vellum Copies and 300 on
Hand-made paper are for sale in England.

No.   130   .

THE KING'S LIBRARY

EDITED BY PROFESSOR GOLLANCZ, LITT.D.

THE DE LA MORE PRESS FOLIOS

IV. THE PERCY FOLIO

FROM THE TEXT OF DR. F. J. FURNIVALL
AND PROFESSOR J. W. HALES   VOLUME II

The Publishers and General Editor of "The King's Library" desire to express their thanks to Dr. F. J. Furnivall and Prof. J. W. Hales for kindly allowing the use of their text for the present issue.

LONDON

AT THE DE LA MORE PRESS

1906

CONTENTS OF VOLUME II.

CONTENTS—*continued*

THE PERCY FOLIO

MERLINE

Hee that made with His hand
Both winde, water, and lande,
Give them all good ending
That will listen to my talking!
And I shall you informe
How Merlyn was gotten and borne,
And of his wisdome alsoe,
And other happs many mooe
Which then befell in England.
He that will this understand :   10
In England there was a King,
A noble man in all thinge,
In warr he was ware and wight,
Constantine forsooth he hight ;
A doughtye man he was of deed,
And right wise he was of reede ;
King he was of great honor,
And holden prince and Emperour.
For King Anguish of Denmarke,
And many a Sarazen stoute and starke,   20
Warred on him withouten fayle,
And he overcame them in battaile
That they durst him not abyde,
And drove them out of feild that tyde.
Then had the Kinge sonnes three,
The fairest children that might bee ;
The eledest sonne, that shold be king,
Was called Moyne, without leasing.
The other were of great renowne,
Both Uther and Pendragon.   30

In that time (wee find in booke)
A great sicknesse the King tooke,
That out of this world he must wende;
And after his Barrons he did send,
And wen they were comen everecheone
The King said to them anon,
" Lords," he said to them anon,
" Out of this world must I gon:
For Gods love and charitye,
And for the love you owe to me,   40
When I am dead and locked in clay,
Helpe my children in what you may,
And take Moyne my eldest sonne,
And make him King, and give him crowne;
Hold him for your Lord," said hee.
All they granted itt shold soe bee.
Then had the King a steward fayre
That was called Sir Vortiger;
His truth to the King he plight
To helpe his children with all his might;   50
But soone the traytor was forsworne,
And brake troth he had made beforne.
For the King out of this world went,
And faire was buryed verament;
Att Winchester, without leasinge,
There was made his buryinge.
Erles and Barons soone anon
Tooke them together everechone;
With-out any more dwellinge
They made Moyne Lord and King.   60
But the steward, Sir Vortiger,
Was full wrath, as you may heere,
And stoode there againe with all his might
Both by day and eke by night,
For he thought himselfe with treason
To be Lord and King with crowne.

2

As soone as Moyne was chosen King,
Into Denmarke the word can springe:
King Anguis hard it then,
And therof was both glad and faine;   70
Soone messengers in that ilke tyde
He sent over all the land wyde,
After many Sarazens stout and starke,
And of Saxons, and of Denmarke
A hundred thousand, and yett moe,
On horss backe and on foote alsoe.
Then wold they noe longer abyde;
But dight them to shipp that tyde,
And brought into England, I saine,
Many a doughtye Sarazen.   80
But England was called then
Mikle Brittaine of every man.
Then the word wyde sprange
How the Danish King with wronge
Wrought in England mickle woe.
King Moyne heard that it was soe;
He went unto Sir Vortiger,
And prayed him with lowlye cheere,
And besought him of his honour
For to be his governor   90
Against his foemen to fight.
He answered him anon-right,
And fained himselfe sicke, as traytor strong,
And said with wright and not with wrong,
" He wold never come in battaile
When his strenght began to faile; "
For all this he said aforehand,
For he thought to be King of that land.
The King, he wold him noe more pray,
But tooke his leave and went his way.   100
Messengers he sent that tyde
To all the lands on every side,

3

For erles, barons, and knights
To come and helpe him in his fights.
And when they were all come,
And their armes done upon,
They pricked forth without fayle
To give the Danes King battaille.
There was cloven many a sheeld,
And many knight fallen in feild.   110
All that they mett in strond,
Horsse and man fell to the ground.
Soone the English men, the sooth to say,
Were discomffitt and fled awaye;
To Winchester they ffledden thoe
With much sorrow, care, and woe.
But the Danish King before,
Much of his ffolke he had forlore;
And then forthe he sent his sond
Sone into his owne land,   120
To all that might weapons beare,
Shold come and helpe him in this warre.
Of warre wold he never blinne,
Cytyes and castles for to winne:
In England he warrd full sore
Halfe a yeare and some deale more.
All the barons in England
Took them together in that stond,
What was best for them to done
For to avenge them of their fone.   130
When they were comen all arright,
Erles and barrons, lords and knights,
They said Moyne their young King
Was but a brotherlinge,
And said if Vortiger king were,
He wold bring them out of care;
They said anon, both old and younge,
That Vortiger shold be their King.

4

.

And when they had spoken all this,
Twelve Barrons they send, Iwis,   140
To Sir Vortiger the bold,
To witt whether he nay wold
Against their foemen to stand,
To drive them out of England.
And when the Barrons all in fere
Were come to Sir Vortiger,
Well and hendlyc they him greete,
And on they deske by him they seete;
And bade them with words still
For to say what was their will.   150
And they answered ffayre againe,
And bade that he shold them saine
Why he wold not with them gone
ffor to avenge them of their fone,
And sayden, " Sith Constantine was dead
Wee have had a sorry read ; "
And bade that he shold take in hand
To warre them out of England.
Then answered Sir Vortiger
As a man of great power,   160
" I was yett never your King ;
Why pray you me of such a thinge ?
Nor yett never here beforne,
Nor to you was never sworne
For to helpe you att your neede ;
And therfore, soe God me speede,
Wend home unto your King,
And pray him in all thing
To helpe you against your fone,
For helpe of me gett you none."   170
Then answered a bold Barron,
" Our King is but a younge one ;
For when he seeth a sword drawne,
He weeneth to bee slowen ;

5

Hee doth us noe other good,
But flyeth away as he were wood.
Had thou beene amongst us all,
That chance had never beffalle;
Thus saine all our peeres."
" I trow well," said Vortiger;   180
" Certaine it was great dole
To make a Kinge of such a foole;
Had you made a man your King,
He had saved you in all thinge;
But sithen siker you bee,
Helpe gett you none of mee.
But if your King were dead aplight,
I wold helpe you with all my might."
Then said the Barrons eche one,
" Will yee that wee our King slowen?"   190
" Nay," he sayd, " with-outen strife,
While your younge King is alive,
Helpe gett you none, I-wis."
The Barrons tooke leave with this;
To Winchester they went all
There the King was in halle;
And as he sate att meate
They run to him in great heate;
And as he sate att the bord,
Or ever he spake any word,   200
They run all to him anon
And smitten of his head full soone.
And when the King was thus slowe,
Ereles, Barrons, hye and lowe,
Tooken them all to reede
That a King they must have need,
All England for to warre
Against them that will or darre.
Then had Moyne brethren tow,
Younge children they were alsoe,   210

6

The one hight Uther, the other Pendragon.
Then saiden the Barrons everye one
That they shold never speede
But if a doughtye man of deede
Were chosen to be their King in fere;
And sweren that Sir Vortiger
Was a doughtye man of deede,
Stout and stale-worth of a steede;
They swearen then together eche one,
That other King they wold have none,   220
Then was there neither knight nor swaine
That durst speake them againe,
But granted it, both old and younge,
To make Sir Vortiger their king.
Soe in the time of Aprill, as yee may heere,
The twelve Barrons came to Vortiger,
And said that England's right
Was lorne thorrow their King a-plight,
And he was dead, without leasing,
And his two brothers were to young   230
To hold the kingdome in hand,
" Therfore the commons of the land
Have you chosen with honour
For to be their emperour."
Blithe and glad was Vortyger,
And anon was King without danger.

Second Parte

Att the feast of the turnament
The Barrons that were gent,
That all the treason understoode,
They had ruth of the right blood,   240
That they children shold be done to dead;
Therfore they tooke another reade,

7

And tooken Uther and Pendragon,
And passed over the seas anon.
Of theire passage wist noe moe
But the hend Barrons two.
And when the feast was all hold,
Vortiger the traitor bold
Lett make accompackement
Of erles and barrons that were gent,   250
Att which Parlament they had hight
For to have slaine they children right.
Vortiger commanded anon
For to feitch Uther and Pendragon.
Fast about all they sought,
But they cold find them nought.
When Vortiger this understoode,
Then hee waxed almost woode,
But never-the-lesse Sir Vortiger
Did give commandment far and neere   260
To duke, erle, barron, and knight,
To make them rydey for to fight;
And soone they dight them, I-wis,
With armes and with horsses of price.
And when they were ready dight,
Forsooth it is a seemlye sight:
With helme one head, and bright banner,
All went forth with Vortiger.
The King of Denmarke with pryde
Brought his host by his syde;   270
Either host can other assayle;
There might you see a strong battele.
The English folkes, sooth to say,
They foughten so well that day
That King Anguish in that tyde
Was upon the worsse side,
And ffledd away as he were woode
Into a castle faire and goode;

And manye of his host alsoe,
Fast away can they goe;   280
And Vortiger with his rowte
Besett the castle all aboute.
And when they had long laine,
Vortiger send to them for to saine
If he peace passe must,
Hee wolde take all his host
And wende into his countrye,
And never after that day
Wold he passe the sea stronde,
Ne come to warr in Englande.   290
And when this covenant was all done,
That they wold not into England come,
Vortiger tooke his councell
And lett them passe certaine;
And soe they went to the sea,
And passed to their owne countrye.
Vortiger then tooke his ost
And went thence with a great boaste;
He held feast many a day
With much solace and with play.   300
And when the feast was all helde,
The twelve Barrons that I erst of told,
That had slaine Moyne the King,
They bethought them of a wonderous thing,
That they wold wend to Vortiger
And aske him meede and liverr,
And said, " Vortiger, now you bee above,
Now yeelde us meede! for thy love
Wee slew our right King by kind;
Now will wee see if thou bee hynde;   310
For wee brought thee to thine above;
Thinke what wee did for your love!"
King Vortiger answered againe:
With egar moode he can saine.

c   9

" By the law that God made
You shall have as yee bade!
For yee are traitors starke and stronge,
And have slaine your King with wronge,
And yee have wrought against the law!
And therfore yee shall both hang and draw." 320
He did take horsses fleete,
And tyed them to their ffeete,
And then drew them on a pavement,
And sithen hanged them verament.
Then many an erle and barron hynde
That were of the barrons kinde,
To Vortiger they ran anon
As his most deadlye fone;
Hard on him can they fight,
For to slay him they thought right. 330
Vortiger with might and maine,
He with his host went them againe;
A strong battell there was dight,
And many a head ther of smitt,
Soe that Vortiger that day
Was glad for to scape away.
Anon the Barrons send their sonde
Wyde over all England
To all their ffreinds, sibb and couthe,
East, west, north and southe, 340
And told them that sooth tyde,
How Vortiger with great despighte,
With great treason and with wrong,
Their kinred had drawen and honge.
Wrath then was many a man,
And al together swarren then
That they wold not assunder breake
Till they were on him wreake.
Everye man on other besought,
A great host on him they brought, 350

And foughten with Sir Vortiger
Nine monthes of this yeere,
That many a lady fayre and free
Lost her lord and her meanye.
Then the warr endured long,
And the Barrons waxed strong
That Vortiger had not power
Against them longer to endure.
Messengers anon hee tooke,
And made them sworne upon a booke 360
That they shold his arrand gone;
And letters he tooke to them anon,
And sent them over the seas, I-wis,
To Denmarke, unto King Anguis,
And that hee shold come att neede
With all the power that he might lead,
Against his foemen for to fight
That wold deprive him of his right.
Then was King Anguis blythe,
And messengers hee sent swithe 370
To duke, erle, barron, and knight,
And to all that weapon beare might.
Then to shipp they went blithe,
And over the sea can they drive;
And when they came to Vortiger,
He welcomed them with merry cheere,
And seazed there into his hands
Halfe the realme of England
That he had, or have might,
For to helpe him in his right. 380
When this covenant was made fast,
All they dighten them in hast
Into battelle for to wend
With the Barrons that were hende;
Besids Salsbury a lyte,
There the battell can they smite.

11

Many a bold champion,
And many a thousand, in that stonde
Were slaine and brought to ground;
Many a ladye and damsell 390
Can weepe that day with teares fell.
Then had Vortiger ten
Against one of the Barrons men;
Discomffitted they were that day;
With great sorrow they fled away;
And Vortiger, that wold not spare,
But hunted them as hound doth hare,
Them that he did overtake,
Noe other peace did he make,
But did them all to-draw and hange. 400
But sithen all that was wrong;
Many a Barron hynde and free
Fled out of his owne countrye,
And dwelled out many a yeere
For love of Sir Vortiger.
Then Vortiger ceazed into his hands
The lands and rents of all the Barrons;
And both wiffe, chyld and swaine,
He drove out of the lannd certaine.
King Anguis had verament 410
A daughter that was faire and gent,
That was heathen Sarazen;
And Vortiger for love fine
Undertooke her for his wiffe,
And lived in cursing all his liffe,
For he did make the Christen men
To marry the heathen women,
Soe that nighe all England
Was fallen into the devills hand;
And thus they lived many a yeere. 420
Soe on a day Sir Vortiger
Bethought him on the children tow

That out of the land were fledden thoe,
And alsoe he bethought him then
Of many another doughtye man
That hee had fleemed out of the land,
And in his hart gan understand
That it was a sorry happe,
And doubted him of an afterclappe.
Anon he sent messengers   430
Over all the land for carpenters,
And for good massons alsoe,
The best that were in land thoe.
Many a thousand there came anon
That colde worke lime and stone;
And when they were comen all,
The King anon to them gan call,
And said, " Lordings, I have thought
A strong castle to be wrought
Of bigge timber, lime, and stone,   440
That such another be noe-were none,
If ever I have any need,
My liffe therin that I may lead.
The castle yee shall make surlye
Upon the Plaine of Salsburye;
Goe and doe as I you bade,
That itt be surlye and well made,
And you shall have to your hyer
As much as you shall desire."
The workemen went forthe thoe,   450
Fifteen thousand and yett moe,
Hewen timber, carving stone,
And laid a foundation there anon.
Some laid, and some bore,
And some can the worke arreare.
That ilke day, round about
Itt was brest high without doubt.
When itt came to the night,

To their bedd they went wright,
And came againe upon the morrow 460
And found a thing of much sorrow,
For all the fondation they found
Lying abroad upon the ground,
And all to-torne, both lime and stone.
They had great wonder, everye one:
Better read then cold they none,
But began it new againe,
And sped as well, the sooth to say,
As they did the first daye.
And when the evening was comen, 470
They went to bedd all soone.
On morrow they came anon,
And found it cast downe, lime and stone,
And was spredd both heere and there;
And thus they faren halfe a yeere.
When the King heard of this,
Great wonder he had, I-wis,
And oft asked both young and old,
And of the wonder wold be told,
And why the worke might not stand. 480
There was none within the land,
Highe nor lowe, learned nor clarke,
That cold tell him of the worke.
King Vortiger sate in his hall
Amongst his barrons and knights all,
And sware he wold never spare
Untill he wist why it were;
And anon he sent his sonde
Over all England
After clerkes old and younges 490
That cold tell him wonderous things.
The messengers forth went,
And did the Kings comandement;
Many a wise clarke they sought;

Before the King they all were brought.
King Vortiger opposed them all
Why his worke did downe fall;
But there was none that cold him tell.
Then he sware he wold them quell
But if they wold say in hast   500
Why this worke was downe cast.
Ten masters he tooke anon,
The wisest of them every one;
Into a chamber they were doe
That noe man might come them to.
Soe one day verament
They looked into the firmament,
And under the welkin their shewed a skye
That shewedd them witterlye
That in five winters there beforne   510
A knave child there was borne,
Begotten without any man;
And if they had that child then,
And sley him hastilye then,
Or he spoke to any man,
And smeere the worke with his blood,
Then shold that worke be sure and goode:
Thus the sky shewed them there,
And passed away without more.
Then were the clarkes gladd and blythe,   520
And came to Vortiger sithe,
And told him without lesse
Of a knave child that was gotten, I-wis,
Without seede of any man:
Thus they saydden everye one,
' Doe send and feitch that child
Whether hee bee in towne or feild;
And doe him slay hastilye,
And take the blood of his bodye
And smere the worke rond about,   530

15

And it shall stand without doubt.'
Glad and blithe was Vortiger,
And called to him twelve messengers,
And parted them in veritye,
That never a one might other see;
He sent them forth upon his sond
Unto four parts of England,
And commanded that they stint nought
Till he were befor him brought.
Anon the messengers forth went   540
And did the Kings commandement;
And Sir Vortiger the bold
Caused the clarkes to be hold
Till the messengers came againe,
To witt what they wold saine,
And sware by Jesu, heaven King,
If they made any leasinge,
Noe ransome shold for them gone,
But they shold dye everye one.
Now let us tell of these messengers   550
That went from Sir Vortigers
For to seeke the child soe younge;
And yee shall heare a wonderous thing
And if yee will a stond dwell;
Of that chyld I shall you tell,
On what manner the messenger
Brought him to Sir Vortiger,
And what hee hight withouten lesse,
And of what kind he is,
That yee may understand and witt   560
Thorrow what skill he was gett.

Third Parte

David the prophet, and Moyses,
Wittenesse and saith how itt was

That God had made thorrow his might
Heaven full of angells bright:
The joy that they hadden then,
Forsooth no tounge tell can,
Till Lwcifer, with guilt of pryde,
And all that held with him that tyde,
Such vengeance God on them can take   570
That they are now feinds blake.
And I find in holy ritt,
They fell from heaven to hell pitt
Six dayes and seven nights,
As thicke as hayle in thunder lights;
And when it was our Ladyes will,
Heaven closed againe full still.
The feendes that I told of ere,
Fellen out of heaven with Lucifer;
Those that bidden on the ayre on haight,   580
Fell they beene, stronge and sleight;
Of they ayre they take their light,
And have great strenght and might
After man to make a bodye
Fayre of coulour and rudye,
Discending downe among mankind
To tise men to deadlye sinne.
All they wist well beforne
That Jesu wold on Mary be borne;
Therto the feendes hadden envye,   590
And said to the earth they wolden hye
To neigh on earth a maiden mild,
And begett on her a child.
Thus they wend the world to have filed,
But att the last they were beguiled:
I shall you tell how itt was;
Now yee may heere a wonderous case.
In that time, I undestand,
A rich man was in England,

And had a good woman to his wiffe,   600
And lived together a cleane liffe;
A sonne they had, and daughters three,
The fairest children that might bee.
Anon a feende that I of told,
That woonen in the ayre soe bold;
And for to tempt that good woman
He light on the earth then,
And in her body had great might,
And brought her into striffe and fight,
And made her after with egar moode   610
To cursse her child as shee was woode.
Upon a day att even late,
Thorrow the feend, with great hate
With her sonne she gan to grame,
And curst him fast by his name,
And to the devill shee him behight
With all her power and her might.
Then was the feende glad and blythe,
And thought to doe him shame swithe;
And when it was come to night,   620
The feende went to her house right,
And strangled her sonne where he lay.
The wiffe rose up when it was day,
And found her ssonne dead att morrow,
And went and strangled her selfe for sorrowe;
And when her lord heard this,
Anon swithe for sorrow, I-wis,
Sodainlye he dyed thoe
Without shrift or houzell alsoe.
The folke of the cuntrye that tyde,   630
That wooned there neere beside,
Came together then to see,
And had ruth and great pittye,
And many a man that day
Weeped, and sayd " well-awaye "

For that good man and his wiffe
That had lived soe good a liffe!
An hermitt, that wooned there beside,
Came to see them there that tyde—
Blasye forsooth his name was—   640
And oft for them he sayd "alas!"
That it was beffallen soe,
In his heart he was full woe,
And said it was verament
Thorrow the ffeendes incomberment.
The daughters he found there alive;
The hermitt hee can them shrive;
And when he had done and sayd,
Fayre penance on them he layd;
And when hee had done soe,   650
Home again can he goe.
Then the maydens all in fere
Served God with blythe cheere.
In all England then was the usage,
If any woman did outrage
(But if itt were in her spousage),
If any man old or younge
Might it witt of that countrye,
All quicke shee shold dolven bee,
But if it were a light woman called   660
To all men that aske her wold.
Soe the ffeend that had might,
That wooned in the ayre light,
Into the earth he light downe then,
And went unto an old woman,
And hight her both gold and fee
To wende to the sisters three,
The eldest mayden to enchant,
Some younge mans body to enfante;
And shee might bring her therto,   670
He hett her gold for ever-mo.

That old queane was full glad,
And did as the devill her badde,
And went to the sisters three.
As soone as shee might them see,
To the eldest sister soone she saiyd
" Alas, my deere sweete mayd!
Thou hast fayre feete and hande,
A gentle body for to sounde,
White hayre and long arme; 680
I-wise it is much harme
That thy bodye might not assay
With some younge man for to play,
That yee might find in every place
Game, mirth, and great solace."
" Certaine," said the maiden then,
" If that I take any man,
But if it were in spousing,
Any man either old or younge,
And itt were knowen in this countrye, 690
All quicke I shold dolven bee."
" Nay, certaine," said the old queane,
" Yee may it doe without deane
Both in bower and in bedd,
Although noe man doe you wedd;
And therfore dread thee nought,
For it needs never be forth brought;
And if thou wilt doe by my read,
Thou diddest never a better deede."
Soe thorrow the queanes inchantment 700
And the feends incumberment,
The eldest sister, the sooth to say,
Lett a young man with her play;
And when shee liked best the game,
It turned her to much shame,
For shee was taken and forth drawen,
And of her game shee was knowen,

And for that worke dolven was.
Many a man sayd for her "alas!"
The ffeende yett another while   710
The other sister he can beguile,
And made her to love a faire young man,
And after was his lemman then.
Shee was taken forth-wise,
And brought before the hye Justice
Her judgment to understand,
As itt was the law of the land.
The Justice opposed her thoe
Wherfore shee had done soe;
Shee answered as shee was taught,   720
And said shee forsooke itt nought,
And said shee was a light woman
To all that wold come to her common;
And soe shee scaped them away,
Soe that her followed all that day
Of harlotts a great race
To fyle her body for that case.
Yett the feende in that while
The third sister can beguile.
Then was the youngest sister soe woe   730
That nye her hart burst in tow,
For her mother had hangd her selfe,
And her one sister quicke was delfe,
And for that her father dyed amisse,
And her brother was strangled, I-wis,
Her other sister a whore stronge,
That harlotts was ever among;
Almost for sorrow and for thought
In wan-hope shee was brought.
To the hermitt shee went then,   740
To that hight Blassye, that good man,
And told him all the sooth beforne,
How all her kindred were forlorne.

The hermitt had wonder great;
On Gods halfe he her besett,
"I bid thee have God in thy mind,
And let be the lore of the feende,"
And bade her 'forsake in any wise
Pryde, hate, and covetise,
Alsoe sloth and envye,   750
And mans flesh in lecherye,
All such workes for to flee;'
And bade her 'Gods servant bee,'
And bade her to 'take good keepe
That shee layd her not downe to sleepe,
And namelye not in the night,
Unlesse shee had a candle light,
And windowes and dores in that stond
To be spurred to roafe and ground,
And make there againe with good noyce   760
The signe of the Holy Crosse.'
And when he had taught her soe,
Home againe can shee goe,
And served God with hart glad,
And did as the hermitt her bade;
And yett the feend thorrow envye
Beguiled her with treacherye,
And brought her into a dreerye cheere:
I shall you tell in what manner.
Upon a day verament   770
With neighbors to ale shee went;
Long shee sate, and did amisse
That drunken shee was, I-wis.
Her other sister that I of told,
That was a whore stout and bold,
Came thither that same day
With many harlotts for to play,
And missaide her sister as shee was wood,
And called her other then good,

Soe long shee chidd in a resse,   780
The whore start up without lesse,
And went to her sister in a rage,
And smote her on the visage.
Then home to her chamber shee can goe,
And made to the dores betweene them tow,
And cryed out; and neighbors came,
And the whore soone they name
And droven her away anon,
And the harlotts everye one.
When they were driven away,   790
The maid that in the chamber lay
All made, as shee were woode,
Weeped and fared as shee were with ill moode.
And when it was come to night,
Upon the bed shee fell downe right,
All both shodd and cladde;
Shee fell on sleepe, and all was madd,
And forgott her howse unblessed,
As the hermitt had her vised.
Then was the ffeende glad and blythe,   800
And thought to doe her shame swithe;
Over all well hee might,
For there was noe crosse made that night.
And to the mayd anon he went,
And thought all Christendome to have shent;
A traine of a childe he put in her thoe,
And passed away where hee cam froe.
And when that woman was awaked,
And found her body lying naked,
And shee grope with her hands,   810
And some seed there shee found,
Wherby shee wende witterlye
That some man had lyen her by.
Then shee rose up in hast,
And found her dore sparred fast.

23

When shee found that it was soe,
In her hart shee was full woe,
And thought it was some wicked thinge
That wold her to shame bringe.
All the night shee made great sorrowe,   820
And to the hermitt shee went att morrowe,
And told him all the case.
The hermitt sayd, ' alas! alas!
That shee had broken her pennance ; '
And said it was the ffeends combrance.
" A! good father!" said shee thoe,
" What if itt be fallen soe
That a child be on me gotten,
And any man may it witten,
Then shall I be delven anon   830
All quicke, both bodye and bone."
" Certaine," said the good man,
" My deere daughter, after then
I shall you helpe with all my might
Till of itt I have sight.
Goe home, daughter, now, mine,
And have Gods blessing and mine,
For He may—and His will bee—
Out of thy sorrow bringe thee."
Home shee went with dreerye moode,   840
And served God with hart good ;
And everye day after then
Her wombe will greater began
Soe that shee might it not hyde,
But itt was perceived in that tyde.
Then was shee taken forsoothe, I-wisse,
And brought afore the hye Justice.
The Justice opposed her thoe
Why shee had done soe ;
And for shee wrought against the law,   850
He judged her for to be slowe.

And shee answered and said, " nay,
I wrought never against the lay,"
And sware by Him that dyed on tree,
" Was never man that neighed mee
With fleshly lust or lecherye,
Nor kissed my body with villanye."
The Justice answered anon,
" Dame, thou lyest, by St. John!
Thy words beene false and wylde,   860
When men may see thou art with childe!
In this world was never childe borne
But mans seede there was beforne,
Save Jesu Christ thorrow His might
Was borne of a Mayden bright.
How may thou for shame then
Say thou had never part of any man,
When I myselfe they soothe may see
That a child is gotten of thee ? "
" Certaine, sir," shee said then,   870
" I goe with child without any man.
By Him," shee said, " that made this day,
There was never *man* that by me lay ;
But as I sleeped one night,
By mee lay a selcoth wight ;
But I wist never what it was,
Therfore I doe me in thy grace."
The Justice said with-outen fayle,
" I never hard of such a marveil!
To-day nay shall the woman be delfe   880
Till I have asked wiffes twelve
If any child may be made
Without getting of manhood ;
And if they say itt may soe bee,
All quitt shalt thou goe, and free ;
And if they say that it may nay ;
All quicke, men shall delfe thee to-day."

E   25

On twelve wives shee did her anon,
And they answered every one,
That " never child was borne of maiden   890
But Jesu Christ," they all saydden.
Blasye the hermitt upstart then,
To answer the Justice he began;
" Sir Justice," he sayd thoe,
" Hear me in a word or tow:
That this woman hath told eche deale,
Certez, I beleeve itt weele;
And yee beleeven her right nought.
By God and all this world wrought,
I have her shriven and taught the law,   900
To mee wold shee never a-know
That any man for any meede
Neighed her body with fleshlye deede;
Therfore it is against the lay
That shee dolven shold be this day.
Giff shee have served for to spilt,
The chylde in her wombe hath not gilt;
Therfore, sir, doe by my reade,
And put her not this time to dead,
But doe her in warde before   910
Till the childe be bore;
And then," he sayd, " God itt wott,
Two yeere keepe it shee motte,
And peradventure," he sayd, " then
The child may prove a good man."
Then said the Justice,
" Hermitt, thy words are full wise;
Therfore by thy doome I will;
Noe man to-day shall her spill."
They Justice commanded anon   920
To lead her to a tower of stone,
And that noe wight shold with her goe
But a midswiffe, and noe moe.

The tower was strong and hye,
That noe man might come her nye;
A window there was made thoe,
And a cord tyed therto
To draw therein all thinke,
Fire and water, meate and drinke.
And when the time was comen, 930
Shee bare a selcoth sonne.

Fourth Parte

Right faire shape he had then,
All the forme that fell for a man;
Blacke he was without lase,
And rough as a swine he was.
Then they midwiffe anon-right
Was afeard of that sight;
And for he was soe rough of hyde,
ffull well shee wist that tyde
That he was never gotten by any man, 940
And full faine shee wold then
In hell that he had beene her froe,
That never man had seene him moe.
The hermitt that hight Blassye
Wist full well sikerlye
The time the child shold be borne,
And to the tower he came att morne,
And called upward to them yare,
And asked them how they did fare.
They midwiffe said without lesse 950
A knave child there borne was.
"Take him me," he sayd then,
"And I shall make him a Christen man;
Whether he dye, or live abyde,
The fairer grace he may betyde."

27

Full glad was the midwiffe,
And caught the chyld be-live,
And by a cord shee lett him downe,
And Blassy gave him his benison,
And bare him home with merry moode,   960
And batptized him in the holy floode,
And called him to his christendome,
And named him Merlyin in Gods name.
Thorrow that name, I you tell,
All the ffeends that were in hell
Were agreeved, and that full sore;
Therfore was their power bore.
And when he had christened him soe,
Home againe he bare him thoe,
And in the cord he can him laine;   970
The midwiffe drew him up againe,
And he bade her without blame
Call him Merlyne by his name.
The midwiffe bare him anon-right
To the ffyer that was bright,
And as shee warmed him by the fyer
Shee beheld this lodlye cheere:
"Alas," said shee, "art thou Merlyn?
Whence art thou, of what kinne?
Who whas thy father by night or day?   980
That noe man I-witt itt may.
It is great ruth, by Heavens King,
That for thy love, thou foule thinge,
Thy mother shalbe slaine with woe!
Alas the time it shalbe soe!
I wold thow were farr in the sea,
That thy mother might scape free!"
When Merlyn hard her speake soe,
He bradde open his eyen towe,
And lodlye on her can hee looke,   990
And his head on her hee shooke,

And gan to cry with lowd dinne:
" Thou lyest," he sayd, " thou foule queane!
My mother," he sayd, " shall noe man quell
For nothing that men can tell;
Whilest I may speak or gone,
Mauger them that wold her slone,
I shall save her liffe for this;
That you shall see and heare, I-wis."
When the midwiffe shee heard that,   1000
Shee fell downe almost flatt;
Shee gan to quake as shee were wood,
And had rather then any good
That shee had beene farr away;
Soe had his mother where she lay;
Soe sore they were of him agast,
They blessed them, and that full fast,
And cryed on him in Gods name
That he shold doe them noe shame;
And fast on him they can crye   1010
In Gods name and St. Marye
He shold them tell what hee were,
And what misadventure brought him there.
He did lye and held him still,
And lett them crye all their ffill;
And if they shold have slaine him tho,
He wold not speake a word moe.
And they three lived there
With much sorrow and with care;
And for after halfe a yeere,   1020
As shee held him by the fyer,
Rufullye shee gan to greete,
And said to him " my sonne sweete,
For thy love, with-outen weene,
All quicke dolve shall I beene."
He answered and said, " Nay,
Dame, thou gables, by this day;

There is neither man nor Justice
That shall yee deeme in noe wise
Then whilest I may either goe or speak,   1030
In earth thy body for to wreak."
Then was his mother a blythe woman
And everye day after then
He made her gladd and bold,
And marvelous tales to her he told.
When he cold speake and gone,
The Justice was ready anon,
And bade bring forth anon then
Befor him that ilke woman
For to receive her judgment.   1040
And when shee came in present,
The Justice forgatt itt nought,
But egerlye he said his thought,
And sware anon by Heavens Queene
All quicke shee shold dolven beene.
Then the childe answered with words bold——
And he was but two yeeres old——
He sayd to the Justice with egar moode,
"Sir Justice! thou can but litle goode
To doe my mother to the dead,   1050
And wotts not by what reade,
Save a chance that to her ffell;
Therfore thou dost not to her well;
For everye man will wott well then
That against chance may be noe man,
And thorrow chance I was begott;
Therfore everye man may well wott
That my mother ought nought
For my love to death be brought."
Great wonder had both old and younge   1060
Of the childs answering.
Then the Justice was ffull wrath,
And on loud sware an oathe,

All quicke shee shold dolven bee.
" Nay! " said Merlyn, " soe mote I thee,
Thou shalt her never bring therto
For ought that ever thou canst doe!
It shall not goe as thou wilt,
For shee hath done no guiltt,
And I shall prove itt through skill,   1070
Mauger of them that wold her spill.
My father that begatt mee
Is a feende of great potencye,
And is in the ayre above the light,
And tempts men both day and night;
And therfore to my mother he went,
And wend all Christendome to have shent,
And gott mee on her with-out leasinge,
And shee therof wist no thing.
And for shee wist not when it was,   1080
I prove that shee is guiltlesse;
For all the feends wenden by mee
To have shent all Christentye,
And had of me a wicked ffoode;
But God hath turned me to goode;
For now I am of God sende
For to helpe all Englande;
And forsoothe," hee said then,
" Pardie, tell you I can
All that ever was and now is.   1090
I can you tell well, I-wis,
Thou dost not wott, Justice, then,
Who was thy father that thee wanne;
And therfore I prove that mother thine
Rather to be dolven then mine."
Hearknen now all the striffe
How Merlyne saved his mothers liffe!
Then was the Justice in hart woe,
And to Merlyne he said thoe

"Thou lyest!" he sayd, "thou glutton!   1100
My father was a good barron,
And my mother a ladye free;
Yett on live thou may her see."
"Sir," said Merlyne then anon,
"Saynd after her full soone,
And I shall make her to be knowen,
Or else hange me on to drawen."
The Justice after his mother sent;
And when shee was comen present,
The Justice before them all   1110
To Merlyn can he call;
He said to him, "Belanye,
Be now soe bold and hardye
To prove thy tale, if thou can,
That thou saidest of this woman."
Merlyn said to the Justice,
"Sir, thy words be not wise;
If I tell theese folke beforne
How thow was gotten and borne,
Then shold it spring wyde and broad, 1120
And thou shold lose thy manhood;
Then shall thy mother dolven bee,
And all were for the love of thee."
The Justice then understoode
That Merlyn cold mikle good;
Then to a chamber can they goe,
He and Merlyne, and noe moe.
"Merlyn," he said, "I pray thee,
What was that man that begatte me?"
"Sir," he said, "by St. Simon,   1130
It was the parson of the towne!
Hee thee gott, by St. Jane,
Upon this woman that is thy dame."
The lady said "thou fowle thinge!
Thou hast made a starke leasinge!

His ffather was a noble baron,
And a man holden of great renowne;
And thou art a misebegott wretch;
I pray thee God devill thee feitch!
In wyld fyer thou shalt be brent,   1140
For with wronge thou hast my shent."
" Dame," sayd Merlyn, " hold thee still,
For itt were both right *and* skill,
For I wott withouten weene
Thou deserve dolven to beene;
ffor sithe thou was to this world brought,
All the worke that thou hast wrought,
I can tell itt everye word
Better then thou, by our Lord,
How thy sonne was begotten.   1150
Dame, if thou have forgotten,
I can tell you all the case,
How, and where, and when itt was,
And thou shalt be ashamed sore;
Thee were better speake noe more."
The Lady was sore dismayd,
And Merlyn forth his tale sayd:
" Dame," he said verament,
" That time thy lord to Carlile went,—
Itt was by night and not by day,—   1160
The parson in thy bed lay;
Att thy chamber dore thy lord can knocke,
And thou didest on thy smocke
And was sore afrayd that tyde,
And undidst a windowe wyde,
And there the parson thou out lett,
And he ran away full tyte.
Dame," he sayd, " that ilke night
Was begotten thy sonne the knight.
Dame," he sayd, " lye I ought?"   1170
Shee stood still and sayd nought.

Then was the Justice wrath and woe,
And to his mother he sayd thoe,
" Dame," hee sayd, " how goeth this ? "
" Sonne," shee said, " all sooth, I-wis !
For if thou hang me with a corde,
Hee belyeth me never a word."
The Justice for shame waxes redd,
And on his mother shooke his head,
And bade her in hast wend home   1180
With much shame as shee come.
" Belyve," sayd Merlyn, " send after a spye,
For to the parson shee will her hye,
And all the sooth shee will him saine
How that I have them betraine ;
And when the parson hath hard this,
Anon for shame and sorrowe, I-wis,
To a bridge he will flee,
And after noe man shall him see,
Into the watter start he will,   1190
Liffe and soule for to spill :
And but itt *be* sooth that I say,
Boldlye hang me to day."
The Justice withouten fayle
Did after Merlyns counsayle ;
He sent after a spye bold,
And found itt as Merline told ;
And the Justice, for Merlins sake,
Him and his mother he lett take,
And lett them goe quitt and free   1200
Before the folke of that countrye.
And when Merlin was seven yeere old,
He was both stout and bold ;
His mother he did a nun make,
And blacke habitt he let her take,
And from that time verament
Shee served God with good entent.

34

Fifth Parte

Now let us of his mother fayle,
And turne us to another tale,
And speake wee of the messenger   1210
That wenten from Sir Vortiger
For to seeke Merlin the bold,
To have his blood, as I you told.
Soe three of them came by chance
Into the place where Merlyn was
On playing, as he can goe
With other children many moe.
And as they played in that stead
One of his ffellows him misdeed,
And gan to crye on Merlyn thoe,   1220
" Thou cursed srow, thou goe us froe!
Thou art a fowle thing gotten amisse!
Noe man wotts what thy father is! "
The messengers came fast bye,
And hearden well the child crye:
Soone anon they were bethought
That it was the childe they after sought,
And eche one his sword out droughe.
And Merlin shooke his head and laughe,
" Heere comen the Kings messengers   1230
That have me sought both farr and neere
For to have my harts blood!
Now they thinke itt in their moode
For to slay me this day;
But by my truth, if that I may,
Or that they part away from mee,
Well good ffreinds shall wee bee."
Merlyn anon to them ran:
Hee greetes them fayre, as he well can,
And welcomed the messenger,   1240
And sayes, " Yee come from Sir Vortiger;

35

Me to slay is all your thought,
Therof shall yee speed nought;
And for to beare your King my blood,
That never shall doe him good;
For they that told him that tydinge,
Lyed of me a strong leasing,
And said my blood without wronge
Shold make his castle stiffe and strong."
The messengers had wonder then,   1250
And sayd to Merlyn anon,
" How can thou tell us this privitye?
Tell us the sooth, I pray thee,
That wee may have tokeinge
To avow our tale before our King."
Merlin led them a good pace
Till hee came where his mother was;
Shee told them all the sooth beforne
How Merlyne was gatten and borne,
And of his wisdome and of his reede,   1260
And how hee saved her from deade.
The messengers, as I you tell,
All night there did dwell;
Att morrow, soone when it was day,
They tooke leave to wend awaye;
Alsoe Merlyn that ilke tyde
Rode on a palfray them beside,
And wentt forth all in fere
Towards King Vortiger.
As they thorrow the countrye came,   1270
In a towne their inne they tane,
Soe that Merlyne, as I you tell,
Came there as shoone were to sell.
A great laughter up he tooke;
The messengers fast on him can lookee,
And full soone asked him thoe
Wherfore that he laughed soe.

Then sayd Merlyne, " See yee nought
The young man that the shoone hath bought?
He wendes to live them to weare;   1280
But by my hood I dare well sweare
His wretched liffe hee shall forgoe
Or that he is one gate come to."
The messengers att that tyde,
After that man can they ryde,
And found him dead as any stone
Or that he had a furlong gone.
In that town they dwelled all night :
On morrow, when it was daylight,
They dight their horsses, and made them yare   1290
On theire journey for to fare ;
And as they went on their journey
Thorrow a towne in that countrye,
He came by a church yard ;
He mett a course thither-ward,
With preists and clarkes singing beforne ;
The corpes were on a beere borne ;
Many a man therwith can gone.
Merlyn beheld them everye one ;
A great laughter he uptooke.   1300
The messengers on him can looke,
And asked him with hart free
Why he laughed so hartilye ;
He said, " Amongst these folkes then
I see an old sillye man
That doth sore and fast weepe ;
He ought better to skipp and leape :
And others here goe and singe
That ought better their hands to wringe ;
I shall you tell certainlye,   1310
That you may know the cause whye :
That corse that dead is and cold,
Was a childe of ten yeeres old ;

That ilke preist," he sayd thoe,
" That goeth before and singeth soe,
He was the father that the child begott;
And if he were bethought of that,
He wold his hands wring sore,
And for that child sorrow more;
Now he singeth with joy and blisse   1320
As the chyld had never beene his;
And to see the seely husband
For sorrow and care wring his hands,
Therfore he is a mickle ffoole
That for his foomen maketh dole."
The messengers everiche one
To the chylds mother went anon,
And Merlyn in a litle throw
Made the mother to be know,
Wherfore shee cold not say nay,   1330
But ever prayd them naught to say.
Then were the messengers blythe,
And on their journey ridden swithe.
As they ridden on their way,
It was upon the third daye,
When it was about the prime,
Then laughe Merlyne the third time;
Then asked they all in fere
Why he made such laughing cheere.
Then said Merlyne, I-wisse,   1340
" There-of I laugh, noe wonder is;
For sithe the time that yee were borne,
Such wonder heard yee never beforne;
I shall you tell with-outen othe
That yee shall find trew and soothe.
This ilke day, by my truth,
In the Kings house is mickle ruth
Of the Kings chamberlaine;
For the Queene, sooth to sayne,

Hath lyed on him a leasing stronge;   1350
Therfore shee shall be dead with wronge;
For his chamberlaine is a woman,
And goeth in the clothing as a man;
And for shee is fayre and bright of hew,
The false Queene that is untrew,
Besought her to her lemman dearne;
And shee answered, and can her warne,
And sayd, shee must that game forsake;
For noe comfort shee wold her make;
Therfore the Queene was a foole,   1360
For had shee witt of her toole,
And how short itt was wrought,
Shee wold of love asked her nought.
The Queene forthwith was affrayd,
And wend well to have beene bewrayd,
And thought that shee shold be shent;
And before the King anon shee went,
And sayd that his chamberlaine
With strenght wold have her forlaine.
The King therof was wonderous wrath,   1370
And swore many a great othe
That shee shold both hang and draw:
And that were against the law;
Therfore wend you whome belyve
As fast as yee may drive,
And say to Vortiger the King,
The Queene hath made a strong leasing
Upon his chamberlaine for hate;
Therfor bydd that shee be take;
And search the chamberlaine then,   1380
And he shall find shee is a woman!"
A knight there was both stout and stearne,
And pricked forth the truth to learne,
And he made noe tarrying
Till he came before the King.

39

When hee came into the hall,
Downe on his knees can hee fall,
And said, thorrow many a country he went
" On thy message, as thou us sent,
To seeke a child of selcoth land ;   1390
And such a one have wee founde
That is but five wynters old :
You heard never none soe bolde ;
He is clypped child Merline,
He can tell all mannour of thing ;
Of all that was and now is
He can tell you well, I-wis ;
He can tell you full well
What thing troubles your castell,
Why itt may not stand on plaine,   1400
And alsoe of your chamberlaine
That yee have mentt to draw and hang :
He saith ' forsoothe, itt is for wrong
For to slay a woman
That goeth in clothing as a man ;
And therfore doe as I you sayne,
And doe take the chamberlayne,
And of her bonds yee her unbinde ;
A woman fayre yee shall her finde ;
And but itt be soe, with right lawe   1410
Doe mee to hang and drawe.' "
Vortiger a-wondred was,
And all that hearden of that case.
He commanded his men all
His chamberlayne to bring in all ;
Anon they serched her that stonde,
And a woman shee was founde.
Wrath then was Sir Vortiger,
And asked of that messenger
Who told him he was a woman.   1420
" fforsooth, Sir," hee sayd then,

" Merlyn it was that this can say
As wee rydden by the waye;
For he can tell—and lye nought—
All things that ever were wrought;
And all that ever you can him saine,
He will tell you sooth certaine."
Vortiger was glad and blythe,
And said to the messenger swithe,
" I shall yee give both land and ploughe,   1430
And make yee a man right good enoughe;
Therfore I command anon-right,
Duke, erle, barron and knight,
To dight their horsses, and make them yare
Forth with Vortiger to fare."
Then wold he noe longer abyde,
But leapt to horsse, and forth gan ryde
To speake with Merlyn the younge,
For glad he was of his comminge.
But when it was come to night,   1440
With Merlyne he mett right;
As soone as he can him meete,
With fayre words hee can him greete.
Of many things he spoke then—
Some of them tell I can—
With much joy, and verament
To the Kings court they went,
And were att ease all that night.
And on the morrow when it was light,
To that steede they went by-deene   1450
Where the castle shold have beene.

Sixth Parte

" Sonne," he sayd to Merlin then,
" Tell me, chyld, if thou can,

Why my castle in this stonde
Is everye night fallen to ground,
And why it may stand nought,
Of soe strong things as itt is rought."
Then said Merlyn to the King,
" Yee shall heare a wonderous thing:
Heere in this ground deepe 1460
Is a water strong and steepe;
Under the watter are stones towe,
Much and strong, and broad alsoe;
Beneathe the stones under, the mold,
Tow dragons lyen there fould;
The one is white as milke reeme,
The other red as any gleame;
Grislye they are of sight both,
And fare together as the wrothe;
And everye day when itt is night 1470
They begin a strong fight,
That through the strenght of their blast
The worke they can downe cast;
And if the dragons were away,
Then might they workemen worke everye day,
And make thy worke both strong and still,
And to stand att thy owne will.
Doe now looke, and thou shalt see
That it is soothe that I tell thee."
Vortiger commanded anon 1480
All his workemen everye one—
Fifteen thousand and yett moe—
He bade them looke whether it were soe.
Anon they dolven in the ground,
And a watter there they found:
Amonge them all, the soothe to tell,
They made a full deepe well,
And the watter they brought out thoe;
And when they hadden done soe,

Beneath the watter in the ground   1490
Two great stones there they found.
Many men there they were
The two stones up to reare;
And when they were up hent,
Two dragons there were bent;
Foule they were for to behold;
And found itt right as Merlyn tolde,
The one dragon as red as fyer,
With bright eyen as bason cleare;
His tayle was great and nothing small,   1500
His bodye was unryde with-all;
His shape may noe man tell,
He looked like a feende of hell.
The white dragon lay him by,
Sterne of looke and grislye;
His mouth and throate yawned wide,
The fyer brast out on every side;
His tayle was ragged like a feend,
And upon his tayles end
There was shaped a grislye head   1510
To fight with that dragon redd;
For Merlyn said, forsooth I plight,
Soe grislye they were both in sight,
That when they shold uprise,
Many a man they shall agrise.
Anon they ryssden out of their den;
Then was feard many a man;
Of all the folke there was that tyde,
Durst not one of them abyde.
The redd dragon and the white,   1520
Hard together can they smite
Both with mouth and with tayle;
Betweene them was a hard battele
That they earth quaked thoe;
And lodlye whether waxed alsoe;

43

Soe strong fyer they cast anon
That they plaines therof shone;
Soe they fought, forsoothe to say,
All the long summers day
They never stinted their fighting 1530
Till men to evensong did ringe.
Soe in that time, as I you tell,
The red dragon that was soe fell,
Drave the white from a downe
Into the plaines a great verome,
Till they came into a valley;
And there they rested them both tway,
And there the white recovered his flight
And waxed egar for to fight,
And egerlye with-out fayle 1540
The redd dragon he can assayle;
And there the white with all his might
Hent the red anon right,
And to the ground he him cast,
And with the fyer of his blast
Altogether he brent the red,
That never after was found shread,
But dust upon the ground lay.
And the white went away,
And never sithe that time then 1550
Heard noe man where he became.
Then sayd Merlyn the younge
Among them all before the King,
And said to him with words bold,
"Now is itt sooth that I you tolde?
Itt is soothe; yee may itt see;
Therfore, Sir King, I pray thee,
Doe yee the clarkes afore mee bring
That laid on mee that leasing."
And he asked them, the King beforne, 1560
Why they wold his blood were lorne.

And they answered with words myld,
Dreadfullye beforne the chylde,
And sayden, they saw witterlye
Beneath the welkin a skye,
And shewed him all his begott,
How hee was on earth lote,
And thorrow his blood the Kings castle
Shold stande both strong and weele.
Then said Merlyn thoe,   1570
" Hee was a shrew that told you soe ;
That skye," he sayd, " that showed you that,
He was the father that mee begatt,
And for I serve him not att will,
Therfore he wold my blood spill ;
And for that he hath beguiled you soe,
Sir Vortiger, I pray you thoe,
That yee grant them their liffe ;
All my wrath I them forgive."
The King his asking granted swithe ;   1580
Then were the clarkes glad and blythe ;
Forth they went, both more and mynne,
And with them went Merlyne.
Merlyn was with Vortiger
To his counsell all that yeere ;
Through his wisdome and counsayle
The castle was built strong and well ;
And when the castle was all wrought,
Erles and Barrons the King besought
That he wold know att Merlyn thoe   1590
Why the dragons foughten soe ;
Itt was some tokening, they sayd all,
That some adventure shold befall.
Merlyn was brought befor the King,
And he him asked without leasinge
What that tokening might meane,
The fighting of the dragons keene.

45

Merlyn stoode and made danger.
Then bespake Sir Vortiger,
And sayd, " Merlyn, but thou me tell,   1600
Anon I shall cause thee to be quell."
Then answered Merlyn a-plight
With great wrath anon-wright,
And sayd, " withouten weene
That day shall never be seene;
If thou take thy sword in hand
Me to slay or bring in band,
Yett may thou fayle of all thy fare,
As the hound doth of the hare.
I warne you well, Sir Vortiger,   1610
I give nothing of thy danger!
But if thou wilt find me a borrowe
That thou shalt doe me noe sorrowe,
Then will I tell you all bydeene
The fightinge of the dragons keene."
Then sayd Merlyn to the King,
" Sir, understand well my sayinge;
The red dragon so foule of sight
Betokeneth thy selfe and all thy might;
For through thy false procuringe   1620
Moyne was slaine, the younge King.
Thou see the red dragon the white drove
ffar downe into the grove :
That betoekneth the heyres that thou didst fleame
With wrong out of the realme.
Soe all the folke that with them held
Both in towne and in feilde,
The white dragon doth signiefie;
The right heyres have great envye
That thou holdeth all their land   1630
Against them with much wronge;
Alsoe the white, can you well say,
Recovered his flyght into the valley,

46

And drove the redd dragon againe
Till he came to the plaine,
And to the ground he him cast,
And with the fyer of his blast
All to powder he burnt the redd,
That never of him was found a shread.
That betokens the heyres soe younge 1640
Are now waxen, and succour found,
And are readye with many a knight
Against thee to hold fight.
Into this castle they shall thee drive
With thy child and thy wiffe;
And all beene with thee then,
Into the ground shall the brenn;
And the King, Sir Anguis,
Shall be slaine, and hold noe price;
His kingdome and thine alsoe 1650
Shall doe England mickle woe.
The head upon the white dragons tayle,
That betokens withouten fayle,
The heyres that be trew and good
Shall destroy all thy blood:
Sir Vortiger, this is the tokeninge
Of the dragons fighting!
As I thee say, withouten othe,
Thou shalt it find siker and troth."
Still him stood Sir Vortiger, 1660
And bote his lip with dreery cheere,
And sayd to Merline withouten fayle,
" You must tell mee some counsell
Without any more striffe,
How I may best leade my liffe."
Then Merlyne sayd without weene,
" Thus must itt needs beene,
And therfore soe have I rest:
I can noe read, but doe thy best."

47

Vortiger sayd, " but *thou* me tell,   1670
Anon I shall doe thee quell."
He start up and wold him have wrought;
But where he was he wist nought,
Soe soone hee was away then
That in the hall wist noe man,
Hye noe lowe, swaine nor groome,
That whist where Merlyne was become.
Then went Merlyn hastilye
To the hermitt that hight Blassey,
And told him without leasing   1680
How he had served the King;
And told him without wronge
The fighting of the dragons stronge.
Of the red and of the white
A great booke he did endite,
And told that the red dragon
Betokens much destruction
Through Vortigers kinred, I-wis,
And the heathen King Anguis;
In England shold be afterward   1690
Strong battailes and happs hard.
All that Merline tolde and sayd,
In good writting itt was layd,
Of all the ventures, I understand,
That ever shold fall in England;
But for itt is soe darke a thing
That Merlyn made in his sayinge,
That few men withouten weene
Can understand what itt meane;
But on yee will a stond dwell,   1700
Of other things I will you tell.
Of the hend children tow,
Uther and Pendragon alsoe,
I told, as I you understand,
How they were fleamed out of the land;

Now will I tell you in certaine,
In what manner they came againe
With great strenght and power,
And how he drave Sir Vortiger
Forth into his castle strong 1710
For his unright and for his wronge;
And how they brent him flesh and bone,
And how they can King Anguis slaine,
I will yee tell in what mannour:
Listen now and you shall heere.

Seventh Parte

The merryest time itt is in May;
Then springs the summers day;
Soe in that time, as yee may heere,
The Barrons came to Vortiger,
And said, " My Lord the Kinge, 1720
Wee have brought you heard tydinge
Of Pendragon that is thye foe,
And of Uther his brother alsoe;
They are comen into this land
With many a knight doughtye of hand,
And they will stint nought
Till thou be to ground brought;
They are att Winchester almost;
Therfore send about in hast
To all thy freinds, I thee reed, 1730
For thou had never soe much need."
Up him start Vortigers,
And called to him messengers;
To Winchester he them sent,
And bade them, thorrow his commandement,
' Against Uther and Pendragon
They shold shutt the gates anon;

As they wold his love winne,
They shold not let them come in;
And he wold come anon-right   1740
To helpe them with all his might.'
Other messengers he sent anon
To King Anguis soone,
And bade him 'come to helpe att neede,
With all the folke that he might leade,
For to fight against his fone
That were comen him to slone.'
When King Anguis he was come,
The way to Winchester they nume;
And or they were halfe way there,   1750
Uther and Pendragon comen weare
To Winchester towne soe nye,
And reard their bannors on hye;
Armes they shewed rich there
That had beene their fathers before.
Then the burgesse that they banners knew,
Att the first he can them rue
The death of Constantine the King,
And of Moyne that was slaine soe younge,
And said 'Vortiger was a traitor,   1760
And all that wold him succor;'
And said 'they wold let into the towne
Both Uther and Pendragon,
And ceaze there into their hands,
For they were right heyres of the land.'
They sett open the gates wyde,
And lett Pendragon in ryde,
And Uther his brother alsoe,
And all that came with them two;
And yeelden to them both towne and tower,   1770
And didden them full great honor,
That ever after Winchester then
Great thanke and freedome wan.

When that Vortiger the fell
The sooth tydings hard tell,
That Uther and Pendragon
Were let into Winchester towne,
Then he comanded his men fast
To goe to Winchester in hast.
And when Pendragon under-nome 1780
That Vortiger did thither come,
He cast open the gates wyde;
And all they can out ryde,
And dighten them without fayle
To give Sir Vortiger battayle.
But the English Barrons all in fere
That were comen with Vortiger,
When they can they folke seene
That were some time of their kine,
(With Vortiger was many a knight 1790
That knew the banners anon-right;
Well a hundred there were
That had served their father deere,
And saiden ' Vortiger was false in feild,
And all that ever with him helde '),
To Vortiger they ran soone,
And thought for to have slaine him anon.
They had ment to have slaine him there,
But all too litle was their power,
For against one of them 1800
Vortiger had twenty men
That were comen altogether
With King Anguis thither.
King Vortiger and Anguis
For wrath were neere wood, I-wisse;
He commanded all his route
To besett them all aboute,
And sware there shold scape none,
But they shold all be slaine.

Lance they broke, and shafts they drew, 1810
Many of the Barrons they slew;
But they were strong and wight,
And fought againe with all their might;
For nothing wold they yeeld then,
But slew many a heathen man;
Fast on him they can hew,
But alas, they were to few!
Yett one Baron was soe stronge
That hee scaped out of the thronge;
Hee pricked his steed with great randome 1820
Till he came to Pendragon;
He sayd " thou art heyre of this land,
To my tale doe understand!
For the love of thy brother and thee
Hither I come to helpe thee,
And therfor now are wee shent;
For our good will to thee meant,
King Vortiger and King Anguis,
With many a Sarazen of great price
Shall hew us downe to the ground, 1830
But yee us helpe in this stonde."
Itt was noe reed to bid him ryde:
The folke spurred out on everye syde,
And when they were together mett,
There were strokes well besett:
There fought Uther and Pendragon
As they were woode lyons;
Many a Sarazens head anon
They stroke of by the necke bone.
Many folke that ilke tyde 1840
Were slaine on both syds;
King Vortiger, without fayle,
Was overcome in that battele;
And maugre him and all his
That were with King Anguis,

They were driven soe nye
That into a castle they can flee,
And that was both strong and merrye,
Upon the Plaine of Salsburye.
Pendragon and his brother Uther 1850
Pricked after Sir Vortiger;
And when they to the castle came,
Wylde fyer soone them nume
And cast itt in with a gynne;
And as soone as itt was within,
Itt gann to bren out of witt
That noe man might stanch itt;
And Vortiger, with child and wiffe
That were theere in their liffe,
Beast and man, with lymes and lythe, 1860
Were brenned all forthwith.
Vortiger raigned heere
ffullye the space of seven yeere.
Now pray wee all the Heavens King,
And His Mother, that sweet thinge,
He blesse us all with His hand,
And send us peace in England!

Eighth Parte

Now when Vortiger was brent,
Uther and Pendragon went
For to beseege King Anguis 1870
In his castle soe strong of price,
Wither he was fled for dread and doubt.
And Pendragon with all his rout
Besett him soe on every side
That noe man might scape that tyde.
But King Anguis within that castle
Was bestowed soe wonderous well,

And soe stronglye itt was wrought
That noe man might deere itt nought.
And when they had beseeged him longe
About they castle that was soe stronge,
And when noe man might him deere,
Five Barrons comen there
That had beene with Vortiger,
And told Pendragon and Uther
How Merlyne was begotten and borne,
And how he came the King beforne,
And what words he him tolde
Of the dragons under the mould,
And how the King wold have him slaine,
And noe man wott where he become,
And said, "Sir, verament
And Merline were here present,
Throughe his councell you shall anon
Kinge Anguis over-come."
Pendragon was woundred thoe,
And soe was his brother Uther alsoe,
And sent anon the Knights five
For to seeke Merlyn belive,
And bade them, if they found the child,
To pray him with words milde
To "come and speake with Pendragon
And Uther in his pavillyon,
Him to wishe, and them to reade,
And if hee might, helpe them att neede
For to winne that strong hold,
And he shold have what he wold."
The messengers forth went
To seeke Merlyn with good entent,
And fare and wyde they him sought,
But of him they heard right nought.
Soe on a day the messengers,
As they were sett att their dinners

1880

1890

1900

1910

In a taverne in the west countrye,
With meate and drinke great plentye,—
An old churle, hee came in
With a white beard upon his chine,
And a staffe in his hand he had,
And shoone on feete full well made,
And begunn to crave more,　　　　　　　　1920
And said he was an hungred sore,
And praid them on the bench above
To give him something for Gods love.
And they then sayd, with-out leasinge,
'That he shold have of them nothinge,'
And sayd " if that the churle be old,
He is a stronge man and a bolde,
And might goe worke for his meate
If he itt wold with truth gett;"
And called to him evereche one,　　　　　1930
And bade him trusse and away gone,
And sware by the ruth that God them gave,
He shold drinke with his owne staffe.
Then Merlyn answered yorne
" Fellow," hee sayd, " I am noe churle
I am an old man of this worlde,
And many wonders seene and hearde;
And yee be wretches and younge of blood,
And forsooth can litle good;
And if yee knew as yee nay can,　　　　　1940
Yee shold scorne noe old man;
Yee shold be in the Kings neede,
For old men can thee wishe and reede
Where yee shold find Merlyn the chylde;
Therfore the King was full wilde
To send madmen out off rage
For to goe on such a message;
For Merlyn is of such manner,
If he stood before you here

55

And spake to you right att this dore,   1950
You shold know him never the more;
For thrise this day you have him mett,
And yett yee know him never the bett.
And therfore wend home, by my reed,
For him to find you shall not speed;
And bydd that prince take Barrons five,
And bydde come and speake to Merlyn belyve,
And say that he shall them abyde
Right here by this forrests side."
And when he had said to them this,   1960
Anon he was away, I-wisse,
And there wist none of them
Where this old man was become.
The messengers wondred all
Where the churle was befall,
And all about they him sought,
But of him they heard nought;
For in story it is told,
The churle that was soe stout and bold,
That spake soe to the messengers   1970
As they sate att their dinners,
Forsooth itt was Merline the younge
That made to them this scorninge.
The messenger went soone anon,
And told Uther and Pendragon,
And how the churle to them had tolde
And sware to them with words bold,
And told them how Merlyne the chylde
Was byding in the fforrest wylde,
And bade them take Barrons five,   1980
To come and speake with him belyve;
And sayd Merlyn wold them abyde
Att such a place by the forrest syde.
Pendragon had wonder thoe,
And Uther his brother alsoe.

56

Pendragon bade his brother gent
To the seege to take good tent,
That king Anguis scaped not away
Neither by night nor yett by day
Till they were of him wreake,   1990
For he wold goe with Merlyn speake.
Then Pendragon with Barrons five
Went forth alsoe belyve.
And *when* Pendragon was forth went,
Merlyn anon verament
Wist full well that he was gone,
And to Uther he came anon,—
As itt were a stout garrison
He came to Uthers pavillyon,—
And said, " Uther, listen to mee,   2000
For of thy harme I will warne thee,
ffor I know well with-outen fayle
All King Angrius counsaile;
For he will come this ilke night
With many a man full well dight,
And into the forrest slippe anon
For to waite thee for to sloen;
But herof have thou noe dowbt,
But warne thy host all about
That they be armed swithe and weele   2010
Both in iron and eke in steele,
And gather to-gether all thy host,
And hold yee still with-outen bost
Till that hee bee amonge ye comen,
For he shalbe the first groome
That shall upon thy pavillion ren;
And looke that thou be ready then,
And heard on him looke thow hewe,
And spare not that old shrewe,
For thou shalt slay him with thy hand, 2020
And winne the price from all this land."

I   57

And when he had told him all this case,
He vanished away from that place.
Great wonder had Uther thoe
That he was escaped soe,
And thought itt was Gods sonde
That warned him that stonde,
That had soe warned him of his fone,
And was soe lightlye from him gone.
And when itt drew unto the night,   2030
King Anguis anon-right
Did arme his men wrath and prest,
Three thousand men of the best,
And said how a spye had tolde
That Pendragon, the prince bold,
Forth into the countrye is gone,
And left his brother Uther att home;
Therfore, he sayd, he will out breake,
And on other he wold him wreake,
And sware an othe by Mahound   2040
He wold kill him in his pavillyon.
And soone they were ready dight;
Then King Anguis anon-right
Forthe of the castle he can ryde
With three thousand by his syde,
And forthe he went without bost
Untill he came to Uthers host.
And when he was comen right
Where Uthers pavillyon was pight,
King Anguis, a fell felon,   2050
He hyed him to the pavillyon
And thought to slay Uther therin;
But he was beguiled thorrow Merlyine,
For Merlyne had that ilke morrow
Warned Uther of all the sorrow
How King Anguis was bethought;
Therfore in his pavillyon was he nought;

But had taken the feild with-out,
With many a hardye man and stout.
And Uther was a hardy man; 2060
Upon King Anguis hee ran,
And smote him att the first blow
That he cane him over-throwe;
And Uther with his sword soe smart
He smote him thorrow the hart,
And hent him by the head anon,
And stroke itt from the necke bone.
And when the Sarazens this can see,
Fast away can they flee
To the castle ever-eche one, 2070
And left their lord all alone.
But or they might scape againe,
Five hundred were all slayne
Of the stoutest that were there,
That came with their King i-fere.

Ninth Parte

Now let us be for a season,
And let us turne to Pendragon
That was gone to the forrest wilde
To speake with Merlyn the chylde.
The first time he asked for Merlyn, 2080
He see a heardsman keeping swine
With an old hatt upon his head,
And in gray russett was he cladd,
And a good staffe in his hand,
And a white whelpe him followande;
Stalworth he seemed, and well made.
The prince anon to him roade;

And well fayre he can him fraine
Giff he heard ought of Merlyn,
And whether hee cold tell him any tythands,   2090
Where was his most wininge.
" Yea, sir," he sayd, " by St. Marye,
Right now was Merlyn here with mee;
And thou had comen eare, indeed,
Thou might have found him in that stead;
And if thou can Merlyn ken,
He is not yett far gone;
And therfore ryde forth in this way
As fast as ever thou may,
And on thy right hand rathe   2100
Thou shalt find a verry faire path
That thorrow the faire forrest lyeth,
And in that way thou ryde swithe,
And seekerlye with-outen weene
Soone thou may Merlyn seene."
Then was the prince glad and blythe,
And sped him forth swithe;
And as he hard, soe he itt found,
A well faire path on his right hand.
They turned their horsses evereche one,   2110
And in that path they rydden anon,
And with Merlyn they metten then,
And as itt were a stout champyon,
And bare a great packe on his backe;
And to him the prince full faire spake,
And asked him if hee see Merlyn:
" Yea," said he, " by St. Martin,
A little heere before your sight;
He is not farr, I you plyght.
To you I say by St. John,   2120
He is not yett far gone;
And therfore ryde forth belive
As fast as your horsses may drive,

And yee shall find him in a wyle:
By then yee have rydden a myle,
With Merlyn yee shall meete then,
Or yee shall speake with some other man
That shall you tell full right
Where you shall have of Merlyn a sight."
And when he had thus sayd,   2130
They pricked forth in a brayd;
And by they had rydden a stonde,
As he him said with-out wronge,
He mett with Merlyn on the playne,
As he were a doughtye swaine,
All cloathed in robes soe gay
As it had beene a monkes gray,
And bare a gavelocke in his hand;
His speeche was of another land.
He, when the prince had him mett,   2140
Faire and hendlye he did him greete.
Then the prince was all heavye,
And asked him of his curtesie
If he mett by the way
With chyld Merlyn that day:
"Yea, sir," hee said, "by St. Michaelle,
Merlyn I know verry well;
For right now sikerlye
Merlyin was here fast by;
And had yee rydden a litle bett,   2150
With Merlyn yee might have mett;
But sir, I say with-out othee,
He is a quante boy, for-soothe;
Soe well I know Merlyns thought,
With-out my helpe you find him nought;
And if of him yee will have speech,
Then must you doe as I to you teache:
Att the next towne here beside,
There you must Merlyn abyde,

And in the towne take your ine, 2160
And certainly then child Merlyn
Shall come to you this ilke night,
And there yee shall of him have sight,
And then yee may both lowed and still
Speake with Merlyn all that you will."
Then was the prince blythe and glad,
And pricked forth as he were madd,
And tooke his inne in the towne
As shold a lord of great renowne.
Now may you heare in this time 2170
How Merlyn came the fifth time,
And how he the prince mett,
And on what manner he him grett,
And became to him as councellour:
Hearken to me and you shall heare.
When itt was with-in the night,
Merlyn came to the King full right,
Right in the guise of a swayne
As he was in the forrest seene,
And sayd—as I find in the booke— 2180
" Sir Prince, God send you good lucke!
Loe, I am heere that thou hast sought!
Tell me what is thy thought,
And what thou wilt to me saine,
For I wold heare thee wonderous faine."
Then upstart Pendragon,
And into his armes he him nume;
To bide with him he did him crave,
And what hee wold aske, he should have.
And Merlyn sayd verament 2190
' He wold be att his commandement;
Over all, where-soe he were,
He wold be att his bydding yare.'
Then was the prince gladd and blyth,
And thanked Merlyn many a sythe.

Then sayd Merlyn, " Sir, will you heare?
I come from thy brother deere;
For through my councell hee hath this night
Slaine King Anguis, I you plight."
Then was the prince blythe and gladd, 2200
And great solace and myrth made;
And all that were there were full faine,
And on the morrow rod home againe,
And found King Anguis slaine,
His head sett up, his body drawne.
Pendragon asked Uther, I-wis,
' Who had slaine King Anguis.'
And he answered and can saine
That he *was* warned by a swayne.
When he had told all how he did, 2210
He thanked God in that steade.
Then be-spake Pendragon,
And sayd to Uther anon,
" Hee that thee holpe att need thine,
Forsooth itt was child Merlyn
That standeth now here by thee."
Uther him thanked with hart free,
And prayd him then in all thing
That he wold be att his bidding.
Then they wenten to the castle with-out lesse, 2220
Wherein many a Sarazen was,
That noe man might to them winne
By noe manner of gynne;
And therefore the oste still lay,
Till after upon the third day
Word came from the Sarazen
Where they lay in castle fine,
That they wold yeeld up the castle;
If they might passe well
To their land with-outen dere, 2230
Upon a Booke they wold sweare

That they shold never againe come.
But Merlyn sent them word soone
That they shold pass eache one
By leave of his Pendragon.
And when they had all sworne and some
That they wold never in this land come,
They passed anon to the sea strond
And went into their owne land.
Then to Pendragon the crowne they name,   2240
And King of Englande he became,
And in England he raigned king
But three yeere with-out leasing,
And after he was slaine rathe
With Sarazens, and that was scathe;
I shall you tell in whatt manner;
Listen a while and you shall heare.
That time in the land of Denmarke
Two Sarazens where, stout and starke,
And were of King Anguis kinde,   2250
Of his next blood that was soe hynde;
The one was come of the brother,
And of the sister come the other;
Strong men thew were, and fell,
And theire names I can you tell;
The one was called Sir Gamor,
And the other Sir Malador.
Gamor came of the brother beforne,
The other was of the sister borne,
Great lords were they of land :   2260
Sir Malador held in his hand
Two duchyes, and Gamor three;
Stowter men might none bee.
When they heard how King Anguis
In England was slaine, I-wis,
Altogether can they speake,
Theire unckles death they wold wreake;

And soe great an oste together they brought
That they number they can tell nought;
But unto shipp they gone anon,
And the seas to flowe began.
The winde soe well began to blow
That they landed att Bristowe.
Then Merlyn knew itt well anon,
And told it Uther and Pendragon,
' How there was comen from Denmarke
A stronge oste stout and starke,
With many Sarazens of price,
For to avenge King Anguis.'
" In England," sayd Merlyn then,
" Such an oste was never seene;
I say to you with-outen layne,
The one of you shalbe slayne;
And whether of you soe ere it is,
Shall have to meede heavens blisse."
But for noe meede he wold not saine
Whether of them shold be slaine;
But never-the-lesse yee shall heare.
Merlyn loved well Uther,
The least heere that was on his crowne,
Then all the body of Pendragon.
Hee bade them dight them anon
Against their foemen for to gone,
And sayd ' Pendragon with-out fayle
Uppon the land shold them assayle; '
" And Uther, alsoe I bidd thee,
Thou shalt wend by the sea,
And looke that theere scapen none
Till they be slaine everye-eche one."
Pendragon was a doughtye knight,
And fell and egar for to fight;
He never for stroakes wold forbeare
Against noe man with sheeld or speare,

Nor better did with-outen fayle,
And that was seene in that battaile;
He tooke his oaste with might and mayne,
And went the Sarazens fast againe;
And when they were together mett,
There were strokes sadlye sett;
Many a heathen Sarazen   2310
He clove downe to the chin;
Many a man was sticked tho,
And many a good steed was slayne alsoe.
The booke saith with-outen lye
There was done such chivalrye;
Of the folke that [by] Pendragon fell,
Noe man can the number tell.
And Uther to the sea went,
And Merlyn told him verament
That he shold not that day be slaine.   2320
Then was Uther wonderous fayne,
And in his hart so wonderous lyght
That hee was feirce and fell in fight,
And egerlye with-out fayle
The Sarazens he can assayle,
And fast against them can stryde
That many a Sarazen lost their liffe.
Pendragon and his folke in hast
The Sarazens fast to ground they cast,
That there were none against them stoode,   2330
But fledd away as they were wood.
But Uther in that ilke tyde
Kept them in on the other syde;
With strong battayle and strokes hard
He drove them all againe backward;
And when that they noe further might,
On Pendragon can they light;
A hundred Sarazens on a rowte
Att once layd him all about.

66

Who-soe had seene Pendragon then,   2340
He might have seene a doughtye man;
For all that he might ever reach,
Trulye they need noe other leech.
The Sarazens stout and grim,
Slew his steed under him;
And when hee had lost his steed,
Great ruthe itt is in bookes to reede
How that he on foote stood
Till that he lost his harts bloode.
A hundred Sarazens att a brayd   2350
All att once att him layd,
And broken him body and arme,
And slew him there; and that was harme.
And when that Uither understoode
His brother was slaine, he waxt neere woode,
And bade his men fast fight,
And he bestirrde him like a knight:
Of all the Sarazens that were left alive
There scaped noe more but five.
Of the Christian men were but slane   2360
Three thousand and thirty-one certane;
And in that ilke country thoe
A mile might noe man goe—
Neither by dale nor by downe—
But he shold tread on a dead man.
And when itt was against the night,
Uther had discomfited them in fight;
He went home into his inne,
And asket councell of Merlyne.
Pendragon was out sought,   2370
And to the church full fayre brought;
He was graven and layd full merrye
In the towne of Glasenburye,
And thus ended that doughtye knight.
God grant his soule to blisse soe bright!

And all that done soe for the right,
I pray Jesu for his might
He grant them heavens blisse above!
AMEN, AMEN, for his mothers love!

ffinis

KINGE ARTHURS DEATH

Off Bruite his blood in Brittaine borne,
    King Arthur I am to name;
Through Chrystendome and heathynesse
    Well knowen is my worthy fame.

In Jesus Christ I doe beleeve,
    I am a Christyan borne;
The Father, Sone, and Holy Gost,
    One God, I doe adore.

In the four hundred and ninetieth yeere
    Over Brittaine I did rayne   10
After my Savior Christ His byrth,
    What time I did maintaine

The fellow-shipp of the Table Round,
    Soe ffamous in those dayes,
Wheratt one hundred noble knights
    And thirty sitt alwayes,

Who for their deeds and martiall ffeates—
    As bookes done yett record—
Amongst all nations
    Wer feared throwgh the world.   20

And in the castle of Tyntagill
    King Uther mee begate
Of Agyana, a bewtyous ladye,
    And come of his estate.

And when I was fifteen yeere old,
    Then was I crowned King;
All Brittaine was att an uprore,
    I did to quiett bringe,

And drove the Saxons from the realme,
    Who had opprest this land;   30
And then I conquered througe manly feats
    All Scottlande with my hands.

Ireland, Denmarke, Norway,
    These countryes wan I all,
Iseland, Gotheland, and Swethland,
    And made their kings my thrall.

Five kings of Pavye I did kill
    Amidst that bloody strife;
Besides the Grecian Emperour,
    Who alsoe lost his liffe.   40

I conquered all Gallya
    That now is called ffrance,
And I slew the hardy Froland feild,
    My honor to advance;

And the ugly gyant Danibus
    Soe terrible *to* vewe,
That in St. Barnards mount did lye,
    By force of armes I slew;

And Lucyes, the Emperour of Roome,
    I brought to deadly wracke;   50
And a thousand more of noble knights
    For feare did turne their backes,

Whose carkasse I did send to Roome,
    Cladd poorlye on a beere.
And afterward I past Mountjoye,
    The next approching yeere;

Then I came to Roome, where I was mett
    Right as a conquerour,
And by all the cardinalls solempnelye
    I was crowned an Emperour.   60

One winter *there* I made abode,
    And then word to me was brought
How Mordred, my sonne, had oppressed the crowne,
    What treason he had wrought

Att home in Brittaine heere with my Queene;
    Therfore I came with speede
To Brittaine backe with all my power,
    To quitt that traiterous deede.

And when att Sandwiche I did land,
    Where Mordred me with-stoode;   70
But yett att last I landed there
    With effusion of much blood,

ffor there my nephew Sir Gawaine dyed,
    Being wounded on that sore
That Sir Lancelott in fight
    Had given him before.

Thence chased I Mordred away,
    Who ffledd to London wright;
ffrom London to Winchester,
    And to Cornwalle, hee tooke his flyght;   80

And still I him pursued with speed
    Till at the last wee mett,
Wherby appointed day of fight
    Was agreede and sett,

Where wee did fight soe mortallye
    Of live eche other to deprive,
That of a hundred thousand men
    Scarce one was left alive ;

There all the noble chivalrye
    Of Brittaine tooke their end !   90
O ! see how fickle is their state
    That doe upon feates depend !

There all the traiterous men were slaine,
    Not one escaped away ;
And there dyed all my vallyant knights !
    Alas, that woefull day !

[Second Part]

But upon a Monday after Trinity Sonday
    This battaile foughten cold bee,
Where many a knight cryed well-away !
    Alacke, the more pittye !   100

But upon Sunday in the evening then,
    When the King in his bedd did lye,
He thought Sir Gawaine to him came,
    And thus to him did say :

" Now as you are my unckle deere,
  I pray you be ruled by mee,
Doe not fight as to-morrow day,
  But put the battelle of if you may ;

" For Sir Lancelott is now in France,
  And many knights with him full hardye,   110
And with-in this month here hee wilbe,
  Great aide wilbe to thee."

Hee wakened forth of his dreames :
  To his nobles that told hee,
How he thought Sir Gawaine to him came,
  And these words sayd certainly.

And then they gave the King councell all,
  Upon Munday earlye
That hee shold send one of his heralds of armes
  To parle with his sonne, if itt might bee.   120

And twelve knights King Arthur chose,
  The best in his companye,
That they shold goe to meete his sonne,
  To agree if itt cold bee.

And the King charged all his host
  In readynesse for to bee,
That noe man shold noe weapons sturr
  With-out a sword drawne amongst his knights they
   see.

And Mordred upon the other part,
  Twelve of his knights chose hee   130
That they shold goe to meete his father
  Betweene those two hosts fayre and free.

And Mordred charged his ost
    In like mannor most certainely,
That noe man shold noe weapons sturre
    With-out a sword drawne amongst them they see;

For he durst not his father trust,
    Nor the father the sonne certainley.
Alacke! this was a woefull case
    As ever was in Christentye!   140

But when they were mett together there,
    And agreed of all things as itt shold bee,
And a monthes league then there was
    Before the battele foughten shold bee,

An adder came forth of bush,
    Stunge one of King Arthirs knights below his knee;
Alacke! this was a woefull chance
    As ever was in Christentye!

The knight he found him wounded there,
    And see the wild worme there to bee;   150
His sword out of his scabberd he drew;
    Alas! itt was the more pittye!

And when these two osts saw they sword drawen,
    They joyned battell certainlye,
Till of a hundred thousand men
    Of one side was left but three.

But all were slaine that durst abyde,
    But some awaye that did flee.
King Arthur upon his owne partye
    Himselfe alive cold be,   160

And Lukin the Duke of Gloster,
    And Bedever his Butler certainlye.
The King looked about him there,
    And saw his knights all slaine to bee;

"Alas!" then sayd noble King Arthur
    "That ever this sight I see!
To see all my good knights lye slaine,
    And the traitor yett alive to bee!

"Loe where he leanes upon his sword hillts
    Amongst his dead men certainlye!   170
I will goe slay him att this time;
    Never att better advantage I shall him see."

"Nay! stay here, my leege!" then said the Duke,
    "For love and charitye!
For wee have the battell woone,
    For yett alive wee are but three:"

The King wold not be perswaded then,
    But his horsse then mounted hee;
His Butler that helped him to horsse,
    His bowells gushed to his knee.   180

"Alas!" then said noble King Arthur,
    "That this sight I ever see,
To see this good knight for to be slaine
    For love for to helpe mee!"

He put his speare into his rest,
    And att his sonne he ryd feirclye,
And through him there his speare he thrust
    A fatham thorrow his body.

The sonne he felld him wounded there,
    And knew his death then to bee;   190
He thrust himselfe upon his speare,
    And gave his father a wound certainlye.

But there dyed Sir Mordred
    Presently upon that tree.
But or ere the King returned againe,
    His Butler was dead certainlye.

Then bespake him noble King Arthur,
    These were the words sayd hee,
Sayes, " Take my sword Escalberd
    From my side fayre and free,   200
    And throw itt into this river heere;
For all the use of weapons Ile deliver uppe,
    Heere underneath this tree."

The Duke to the river side he went,
    And his sword in threw hee;
And then he kept Escalberd,
    I tell you certainlye;

And then he came to tell the King.
    The King said, " Lukin, what did thou see? "
" Noe thing, my leege," then sayd the Duke,   210
    " I tell you certainlye."

" O goe againe," said the King,
    " For love and charitye,
And throw my sword into that river,
    That never I doe itt see."

The Duke to the river side he went,
    And the Kings scaberd in threw hee;
And still he kept Escalbard
    For vertue sake faire and free.

He came againe to tell the King;   220
    The King sayd, "Lukin, what did thou see?"
"Nothing, my leege," then sayd the Duke,
    "I tell you certainlye."

"O goe againe, Lukin," said the King,
    "Or the one of us shall dye."
Then the Duke to the river sid went,
    And the Kings sword then threw hee:

A hand and an arme did meete that sword,
    And flourished three times certainlye.
He came againe to tell the King,   230
    But the King was gone from under the tree,

But to what place, he cold not tell,
    For never after hee did him see,
But he see a barge from the land goe,
    And hearde ladyes houle and cry certainlye;

But whether the King was there or noe
    He knew not certainlye.
The Duke walked by that rivers side
    Till a chappell there found hee,

And a preist by the aulter side there stood.   240
    The Duke kneeled downe there on his knee
And prayed the preists, "for Christs sake
    The rights of the church bestow on mee!"

For many dangerous wounds he had upon him,
    And liklye he was to dye.
And there the Duke lived in prayer
    Till the time that hee did dye.

King Arthur lived King twenty-two yeere
    In honor and great fame,
And thus by death suddenlye   250
    Was deprived from the same.

ffinis.

KINGE JOHN AND BISHOPPE

Off an ancient story Ile tell you anon,
Of a notable prince that was called King John,
In England was borne, with maine and with might
Hee did much wrong, and mainteined litle right.
This noble prince was vexed in veretye,
For he was angry with the Bishopp of Canterbury
ffor his house-keeping and his good cheere.
They rode post for him, as you shall heare;
They rode post for him verry hastilye;
The King sayd the Bishopp kept a better house
    then hee;   10
A hundred men even, as I say,
The Bishopp kept in his house everye day,
And fifty gold chaines, without any doubt,
In velvett coates waited the Bishopp about.
The Bishopp, he came to the court anon
Before his prince that was called King John.
As soone as the Bishopp the King did see,
" O," quoth the King, " Bishopp, thow art welcome
    to mee!
There is noe man soe welcome to towne
As thou that workes treason against my crowne."   20
" My leege," quoth the Bishopp, " I wold it were
    knowne;
I spend, your Grace, nothing but that thats my owne;
I trust your Grace will doe me noe deare
For spending my owne trew gotten geere."
" Yes," quoth the King, " Bishopp, thou must needs dye:
Eccept thou can answere mee questions three,
Thy head shalbe smitten quite from thy bodye,
And all thy living remayne unto mee.
First," quoth the King, " tell me in this steade,
With this crowne of gold heere upon my head,   30

Amongst my nobilitye with joy and much mirth,
Lett me know within one pennye what I am worth:
Secondlye, tell me without any dowbt
How soone I may goe the whole world about:
And thirdly, tell mee or ever I stinte,
What is the thing, Bishopp, that I doe thinke.
Twenty dayes pardon thoust have trulye,
And come againe and answere mee."
The Bishopp bade the King ' god night ' att a word.
He rode betwixt Cambridge and Oxenford,   40
But never a Doctor there was soe wise
Cold shew him these questions or enterprise;
Wherewith the Bishopp was nothing gladd,
But in his hart was heavy and sadd,
And hyed him home to a house in the countrye
To ease some part of his melanchollye.
His halfe brother dwelt there, was feirce and fell,
Noe better but a shepard to the Bishoppe him-sell;
The shepard came to the Bishopp anon,
Saying, " My lord, you are welcome home!   50
What ayles you," quoth the shepard, " that you are
     soe sadd,
And had wonte to have beene soe merry and gladd?"
"Nothing," quoth the Bishopp, "I ayle att this time,
Will not thee availe to know, brother mine."
" Brother," quoth the shepeard, " you have heard itt,
That a ffoole may teach a wisemane witt;
Say me therfore what-soever you will,
And if I doe you noe good, Ile doe you noe ill."
Quoth the Bishop : " I have beene att thy court anon,
Before my prince is called King John,   60
And there he hath charged mee
Against his crowne with traitorye;
If I cannott answer his misterye,
Three questions hee hath propounded to mee,
He will have my land soe faire and free,

And alsoe the head from my bodye.
The first question was, ' to tell him in that stead
With the crowne of gold upon his head,
Amongst his nobilitye with joy and much mirth,
To lett him know within one penye what hee is
      worth ; '   70
And secondlye, ' to tell him with-out any doubt
How soone he may goe the whole world about ; '
And thirdlye, ' to tell him, or ere I stint,
What is the thinge that he does think.' "
" Brother," quoth the shepard, " you are a man of
      learninge ;
What neede you stand in doubt of soe small a thinge ?
Lend me," quoth the shepard, " your ministers apparrell,
Ile ryde to the court and answere your quarrell ;
Lend me your serving men, say me not nay ;
With all your best horsses that ryd on the way,   80
Ile to the court, this matter to stay ;
Ile speake with King John and heare what heele say."
The Bishopp with speed prepared then
To sett forth the shepard with horsse and man ;
The shepard was lively with-out any doubt ;
I wott a royall companye came to the court.
The shepard hee came to the court anon
Before *his* prince that was called King John.
As soone as the King the shepard did see,
" O," quoth the King, " Bishopp, thou art welcome
      to me ! "   90
The shepard was soe like the Bishopp his brother,
The King cold not know the one from the other.
Quoth the King, " Bishopp, thou art welcome to me
If thou can answer me my questions three ! "
Said the shepeard, " If it please your Grace,
Show mee what the first question was."
" First," quoth the King, " tell mee in this stead
With the crowne of gold upon my head,

Amongst my nobilitye with joy and much mirth,
Within one pennye what I am worth."   100
Quoth the shepard, "To make your Grace noe offence,
I thinke you are worth twenty-nine pence;
For our Lord Jesus, that bought us all,
For thirty pence was sold into thrall
Amongst the cursed Jewes, as I to you doe showe;
But I know Christ was one penye better then you."
Then the King laught, and swore by St. Andrew
He was not thought to bee of such a small value.
"Secondlye, tell mee with-out any doubt
How soone I may goe the world round about."   110
Saies the shepard, "It is noe time with your Grace
          to scorne;
But rise betime with the sun in the morne,
And follow his course till his uprising,
And then you may know with-out any leasing—
And this your Grace shall prove the same—
You are come to the same place from whence you came;
Twenty-four houres, with-out any doubt,
Your Grace may the world goe round about;
The world round about, even as I doe say,
If with the sun you can goe the next way."   120
"And thirdlye tell me or ever I stint,
What is the thing, Bishoppe, that I doe thinke."
"That shall I doe," quoth the shepeard; "for veretye
You thinke I am the Bishopp of Canterburye."
"Why? art not thou? the truth tell to me;
For I doe thinke soe," quoth the King, "by St. Marye."
"Not soe," quoth the shepeard; "the truth shalbe
          knowne,
I am his poore shepeard; my brother is att home."
"Why," quoth the King, "if itt soe bee,
Ile make thee Bishopp here to mee."   130
"Noe, sir," quoth the shepard, "I pray you be still,
For Ile not bee Bishop but against my will;

For I am not fitt for any such deede,
For I can neither write nor reede."
"Why, then," quoth the King, "Ile give thee cleere
A patten of three hundred pound a yeere;
That I will give thee franke and free;
Take thee that, shepard, for coming to me.
Free pardon Ile give," the Kings Grace said,
"To save the Bishopp, his land and his head;   140
With him nor thee Ile be nothing wrath;
Here is the pardon for him and thee both."
Then the shepard he had noe more to say,
But tooke the pardon and rode his way.
When he came to the Bishopps place,
The Bishopp asket anon how all things was:
"Brother," quoth the shepard, "I have well sped,
For I have saved both your land and your head;
The King with you is nothing wrath,
For heere is the pardon for you and mee both."   150
Then the Bishopes hart was of a merry cheere,
"Brother, thy paines Ile quitt them cleare,
For I will give thee a patent to thee and to thine
Of fifty pounds a yeere land good and fine."
"I will to thee noe longer croche nor creepe,
Nor Ile serve thee noe more to keepe thy sheepe."
Whereever wist you shepard before,
That had in his head witt such store
To pleasure a Bishopp in such a like case,
To answer three questions to the Kings Grace?   160
Whereever wist you shepard gett cleare
Three hundred and fifty pound a yeere?
I never hard of his fellow before,
Nor I never shall.   Now I need to say noe more
I never knew shepeard that gott such a livinge
But David the shepeard that was a king.

ffinis.

MARYE AUMBREE

Captaine couragious, whome death cold [not] daunte,
Beseeged the citye bravelye, the citty of Gaunt!
They mustered their soliders by two and by three:
And the fformost in battele was Mary Aumbree!

When brave Sir John Major was slaine in that fight,
That was her true lover, her joy and delight,
Shee swore his death unrevenged shold not bee;
Was not this a brave, bonye lasse, Mary Aumbree?

The death of her truelove shee meant to requite
With fire and fflamine *and* sword shining bright,   10
Which lately was slaine most villanouslye;
Was not this a brave, bonnye lasse, Mary Aumbree?

Shee cladd her selfe from the top to the toe
In buffe of the bravest most seemlye to show,
And a faire shirt of male slipped on shee;
Was not this a brave, bonye lasse, Mary Aumbree?

A helmett of proofe shee tooke on her head,
And a strong arminge sword shee wore by her side;
A goodly fayre gauntlett on her hand put shee;
Was not this, etc.   20

Shee tooke her sword and her targett in hand,
Bidding all such as wold, wayte on her band.
To waite on her person there came thousands three:
Was not this a brave, etc.

"My soldiers," shee saith, "soe valiant and bold,
Now ffollow your captain which you doe beholde;
In the fight formost my selfe will I bee!"
Was not, etc.

Then cryed out her souldiers, and loude they did say,
"Soe well thou becomes this gallant array,   30
Thy hands and thy weapons doe well soe agree,
There was never none like to Mary Aumbree!"

Shee cheared her good souldiers that foughten for life,
With the cominge of ancyents, with drum and with fife,
That brave sonding trumpetts with ingines soe free,
Att last they made mention of Mary Aumbree.

"Before that I doe see the worst of you all
Come in the danger of your enemyes thrall,
This hand and this sword shall first sett him free;"
Was not, etc.   40

Shee forward went on in battaile array,
And straight shee did make her foes flye away;
Seven houres in sckirmish continued shee;
Was not, etc.

The skyes shee did fill with the smoke of her shott,
In her enemies bodyes with bulletts soe hott;
For one of her owne men, a sckore killed shee;
Was not, etc.

Then did her gunner spoyle her intent,
Pelletts and powder away had he sent: 50
Then with her sword shee cut him in three,
Was not, etc.

Then was shee caused to make a retyre,
Being falsely betrayd, as itt doth appeare ;
Then to save her selfe into a castle went shee ;
Was not, etc.

Her foes they besett her on everye side,
Thinking in that castle shee wold not abyde ;
To beate downe those walls they all did agree ;
Was not, etc.   60

Shee tooke her sword and her targett in hand,
Shee came to the walls, and upon them did stand,
Their daring their captaine to match any three,
Was not, etc.

" Thou English captain, what woldest thou give
To ransome thy liffe which else must not live ?
Come downe quickly, and yeeld thee to mee ! "
Then smiled sweetlye Mary Aumbree ;

" Good gentle captain, what thinke you by mee,
Or whom in my likenesse you take mee to bee ? "   70
" A knight, sir, of England, and captain soe free,
That I meane to take away prisoner with me."

" Good gentle captain, behold in your sight
Two brests in my bosome, and therfore no knight ;
Noe knight, sir, of England, nor captain soe free,
But evene a pore bony lasse, Mary Aumbree."

" If thou beest a woman as thou dost declare,
That hast mangled our soliders, and made them soe bare ;
The like in my liffe I never did see ;
Therfore Ile honor thee, Mary Aumbree."   80

86

" Give I be a woman, as well thou doest see,
Captain, thou gettst noe redemption of mee
Without thou wilt fight with blowes two or three."
Was not, etc.

God send in warrs, such event I abide,
God send such a solider to stand by my side!
Then safely preserved my person wilbe;
There was never none like to Mary Aumbree!

CHEVY CHASE

God prosper long our noble King,
    Our liffes and saftyes all!
A woefull hunting once there was
    In Chevy Chase befall.

To drive the deere with hound and horne
    Erle Pearcy took the way:
The child may rue that is unborne
    The hunting of that day!

The stout Erle of Northumberland
    A vow to God did make,   10
His pleasure in the Scottish woods
    Three sommers days to take;

The cheefest harts in Chevy Chase
    To kill and beare away.
These tydings to Erle Douglas came
    In Scottland where he lay,

Who sent Erle Pearcy present word
    He wold prevent his sport.
The English Erle, not fearing that,
    Did to the woods resort   20

With fifteen hundred bowmen bold,
    All chosen men of might,
Who knew ffull well in time of neede
    To ayme their shafts arright.

The gallant greyhound swiftly ran
    To chase the fallow deere;
On Munday they began to hunt
    Ere daylight did appeare;

And long before high noone they had
    A hundred fat buckes slaine.   30
Then having dined, the drovyers went
    To rouze the deare againe;

The bowmen mustered on the hills,
    Well able to endure;
Theire backsids all with speciall care
    That they were guarded sure.

The hounds ran swiftly through the woods
    The nimble deere to take,
That with their cryes the hills and dales
    An eccho shrill did make.   40

Lord Pearcy to the querry went
    To veiw the tender deere;
Quoth he, " Erle Douglas promised once
    This day to meete me heere;

" But if I thought he wold not come,
    Noe longer wold I stay."
With that a brave younge gentlman
    Thus to the Erle did say,

" Loe, yonder doth Erle Douglas come,
    Hys men in armour bright,   50
Full twenty hundred Scottish speres
    All marching in our sight,

" All pleasant men of Tivydale
    Fast by the river Tweede."
" O ceaze your sportts ! " Erle Pearcy said,
    " And take your bowes with speede,

" And now with me, my countrymen,
    Your courage forth advance !
For there was never champion yett
    In Scottland nor in ffrance   60

" That ever did on horsbacke come,
    And if my hap it were,
I durst encounter man for man,
    With him to breake a spere."

Erle Douglas on his milke white steede,
    Most like a baron bold,
Rode formost of his company,
    Whose armour shone like gold :

" Shew me," sayd hee, " whose men you bee
    That hunt soe boldly heere,   70
That without my consent doe chase
    And kill my fallow deere."

The first man that did answer make
    Was noble Pearcy hee,
Who sayd, " wee list not to declare,
    Nor shew whose men wee bee,

" Yett wee will spend our deerest blood
    Thy cheefest harts to slay."
Then Douglas swore a solempne oathe,
    And thus in rage did say,   80

" Ere thus I will outbraved bee,
    One of us tow shall dye!
I know thee well! an erle thou art,
    Lord Pearcy! soe am I;

" But trust me, Pearcye! pittye it were,
    And great offence, to kill
Then any of these our guiltlesse men,
    For they have done none ill;

" Let thou and I the battell trye,
    And set our men aside."   90
" Accurst bee *he!*" Erle Pearcye sayd,
    " By whome it is denyed."

Then stept a gallant squire forth,—
    Witherington was his name,—
Who said, " I wold not have it told
    To Henery our King, for shame,

" That ere my captaine fought on foote,
    And I stand looking on:
You bee two erles," quoth Witheringhton,
    And I a squier alone,   100

" Ile doe the best that doe I may,
    While I have power to stand!
While I have power to weeld my sword,
    Ile fight with hart and hand!"

Our English archers bend their bowes—
    Their harts were good and trew,—
Att the first flight of arrowes sent,
    Full foure score Scotts they slew.

To drive the deere with hound and horne,
    Dauglas bade on the bent;   110
Two captaines moved with mickle might,
    Their speres to shivers went.

They closed full fast on everye side,
    Noe slacknes there was found,
But many a gallant gentleman
    Lay gasping on the ground.

O Christ! it was great greeve to see
    How eche man chose his spere,
And how the blood out of their brests
    Did gush like water cleare!   120

At last these two stout erles did meet
    Like captaines of great might;
Like lyons moods they layd on lode,
    They made a cruell fight.

They fought, untill they both did sweat,
    With swords of tempered steele,
Till blood a-downe their cheekes like raine
    They trickling downe did feele.

" O yeeld thee, Pearcye! " Douglas sayd,
    " And infaith I will thee bringe   130
Where thou shall high advanced bee
    By James our Scottish king;

" Thy ransome I will freely give,
    And this report of thee,
Thou art the most couragious knight
    That ever I did see."

"No, Douglas!" quoth Erle Percy then,
   "Thy profer I doe scorne;
I will not yeelde to any Scott
   That ever yett was borne!"   140

With that there came an arrow keene
   Out of an English bow,
Who s[t]orke Erle Douglas on the brest
   A deepe and deadlye blow;

Who never sayd more words then these,
   "Fight on, my merrymen all!
For why, my life is att *an* end,
   Lord Pearcy sees my fall."

Then leaving liffe, Erle Pearcy tooke
   The dead man by the hand;   150
Who said, "Erle Dowglas! for thy sake
   Wold I had lost my land!

"O Christ! my verry hart doth bleed
   For sorrow for thy sake!
For sure, a more redoubted knight,
   Mischance cold never take!"

A knight amongst the Scotts there was,
   Which saw Erle Douglas dye,
Who streight in hart did vow revenge
   Upon the Lord Pearcye;   160

Second Parte

Sir Hugh Mountgomerye was he called,
   Who, with a spere full bright,
Well mounted on a gallant steed,
   Ran feircly through the fight,

And past the English archers all
    Without all dread or feare,
And through Erle Percyes body then
    He thrust his hatfull spere

With such a vehement force and might
    That his body he did gore,
The staff ran through the other side
    A large cloth yard and more.

Thus did both these nobles dye,
    Whose courage none cold staine.
An English archer then perceived
    The noble Erle was slaine,

He had *a* good bow in his hand
    Made of a trusty tree:
An arrow of a cloth yard long
    To the hard head haled hee,

Against Sir Hugh Mountgomerye
    His shaft full right he sett;
The grey goose winge that was there-on,
    In his harts bloode was wett.

This fight from breake of day did last
    Till setting of the sun,
For when they rung the evening bell
    The battele scarse was done.

With stout Erle Percy there was slaine,
    Sir John of Egerton,
Sir Robert Harcliffe and Sir William,
    Sir James that bold barron;

170

180

190

And with Sir George and Sir James,
　　Both knights of good account;
And good Sir Raphe Rebbye there was slaine,
　　Whose prowesse did surmount.

For Witherington needs must I wayle
　　As one in [dole]-full dumpes,
For when his leggs were smitten of,
　　He fought upon his stumpes.　　　　　　　　　200

And with Erle Dowglas there was slaine
　　Sir Hugh Mountgomerye,
And Sir Charles Morrell that from feelde
　　One foote wold never flee;

Sir Roger Hever of Harcliffe tow,—
　　His sisters sonne was hee,—
Sir David Lambwell well esteemed,
　　But saved he cold not bee;

And the Lord Maxwell in like case
　　With Douglas he did dye;　　　　　　　　　210
Of twenty hundred Scottish speeres,
　　Scarce fifty-five did flye;

Of fifteen hundred Englishmen
　　Went home but fifty-three;
The rest in Chevy Chase were slaine,
　　Under the greenwoode tree.

Next day did many widdowes come
　　Their husbands to bewayle;
They washt their wounds in brinish teares,
　　But all wold not prevayle.　　　　　　　　　220

Theyr bodyes, bathed in purple blood,
    They bore with them away,
They kist them dead a thousand times
    Ere they were cladd in clay.

The newes was brought to Eddenborrow
    Where Scottlands King did rayne,
That brave Erle Douglas soddainlye
    Was with an arrow slaine.

"O heavy newes!" King James can say,
    "Scotland may wittenesse bee   230
I have not any captaine more
    Of such account as hee!"

Like tydings to King Henery came
    Within as short a space,
That Pearcy of Northumberland
    In Chevy Chase was slaine.

"Now God be with him!" said our King,
    "Sith it will noe better bee,
I trust I have within my realme
    Five hundred as good as hee!   240

"Yett shall not Scotts nor Scottland say
    But I will vengeance take,
And be revenged on them all
    For brave Erle Percyes sake."

This vow the King did well performe
    After on Humble Downe;
In one day fifty knights were slayne,
    With lords of great renowne,

And of the rest of small account,
    Did many hundreds dye :   250
Thus endeth the hunting in Chevy Chase
    Made by the Erle Pearcye.

God save our King, and blesse this land
    With plentye, joy, and peace ;
And grant henceforth that foule debate
    Twixt noble men may ceaze !

ffinis

WHEN LOVE WITH UNCONFINED *WINGS*

When Love with unconfined wings
    Hovers within my gates,
And my divine Althea brings
    To whisper at my grates,
When I lye tangled in her heere
    And fettered with her eye,
The burds that wanton in the ayre
    Enjoyes such lybertye.

When, lynett-like confined, I
    With shriller note shall sing   10
The mercy, goodnesse, majestye
    And glory of my Kinge,
When I shall voice aloud how good
    He is, how great shold bee,
The enlarged winds that curles the floods
    Enjoyes such lybertye.

When flowing cupps run swiftly round
    With woe-allaying Theames,
Our carlesse heads with roses crowned,
    Our harts with loyall flames,   20
When thirsty soules in wine wee steepe,
    When cupps and bowles goe free,
ffishes that typle in the deepe
    Enjoyes such lybertye.

Stone walls doe not a prison make,
    Nor iron barrs a cage;

The spotlesse soule and inocent
  Calls this an hermitage.
If I have freedome in my love,
  And in my soule am free,   30
Angells alone that sores above
  Enjoyes such lybertye!

ffinis

CLORIS

Cloris, farwell!   I needs must goe!
    For if with thee I longer stay,
Thine eyes prevayle upon me soe,
    I shall grow blynd and lose my way.

ffame of thy bewty and thy youth,
    Amongst the rest me hither brought;
But finding fame fall short of truth,
    Made me stay longer then I thought.

ffor I am engaged by word *and* othe
    A servant to anothers will;   10
But for thy love wold forfitt both,
    Were I but sure to keepe itt still.

But what assurance can I take,
    When thou, fore-knowing this abuse,
For some *more* worthy lovers sake
    Mayst leave me with soe just excuse.

ffor thou wilt say it, " it was not thy fault
    That I to thee unconstant prove,
But were by mine example taught
    To breake thy othe to mend thy love."   20

Noe, Cloris, noe! I will returne,
    And rayse thy story to that height
That strangers shall att distance burne,
    And shee distrust thee reprobate.

Then shall my love this doubt displace,
    And gaine the trust that I may come
And sometimes banquett on thy face,
    But make my constant meales att home.

THE KINGE ENJOYES HIS RIGHTS *AGAINE*

What Booker can prognosticate,
Considering now the kingdomes state?
I thinke my selfe to be as wise
As he that gaseth on the skyes;
My skill goes beyond the depth of Pond,
    Or Rivers in the greatest raine,
Wherby I can tell that all things will goe well
    When the King enjoyes his rights againe.

There is neither Swallow, Dove nor Dade,
Can sore more high, or deeper wade   10
To shew a reason from the starres,
What causeth these our civill warres.
The man in the moone may weare out his shoone
    In running after Charles his wayne;
But all is to noe end, for the times will not mend
    Till the King enjoyes his right againe.

ffull forty yeeres his royall crowne
Hath beene his fathers and his owne,
And is there any more nor hee
That in the same shold sharrers bee,   20
Or who better may the scepter sway
    Then he that hath such rights to raine?
There is noe hopes of a peace, or the war to cease,
    Till the King enjoyes his right againe.

Although for a time you see Whitehall
With cobwebbs hanging on the wall,

Insteed of silkes and silver brave
Which fformerly 'twas wont *to* have,
With a sweete perfume in everye roome
    Delightfull to that princely traine :
Which againe shalbe when the times you see
    That the King enjoyes his right againe.

30

ffinis

THE ÆGIPTIAN QUENE

When as the nightingale chanted her vesper,
    And the wyld [forester] coucht on the ground,
Venus invited me to an evening wisper,
    To fragrant feelds with roses crounde,
Which shee before had sent her cheefest complement,
    Unto my harts content sport with me on the greene;
Never Marke Anthony dallyed more wantonly
    With his fayre Ægiptian Queene!

ffirst on her cherry cheekes I my eyes feasted;
    Thence feare of surffetting made me retyre,   10
Then to her warmed *lips*, which when I tasted,
    My spiritts duld were made active by fyer.
This heat againe to calme, her moyst hand yeelded
    balme;
    Whilest wee joyned palme to palme as if wee one
    had beene,
Never Marke Anthony dallyed more wantonly
    With his fayre Egiptian Queene!

Then in her golden heere I my hands twined;
    Shee her hands in my lockes twisted againe,
As if her heere had beene fetters assigned,
    Sweet litle Cupid loose captive to chayne;   20
Soe did wee often dart one at anothers hart
    Arrows that felt noe smart, sweet lookes and smiles
    between.
Never, etc.

Wa[n]*ting a glass to platt* those amorus tresses
    Which like a *bracelet* deckt richly mine arme,
Gaudyer then Juno was which when shee blessed
    Jove with [emb]races more richly thein warme.
Shee sweetely peept in eyne that was more cristalline,
    Which by reflection shine ech eye and eye was
       seene.
Never, etc.   30

Misticall grammers of amorus glances,
    Feeling of pulses, the phisicke of love,
Retoricall courtings and musicall dances,
    Numbring of kisses arithemeticke proves;
Eyes like astronomy, strayght limbes geometry,
    In her harts enginy ther eyes and eyes were seene.
Never, etc.

ffinis

HOLLOWE, ME FANCYE!

In a melancholly fancy, out of my selfe,
Thorrow the welkin dance I,
All the world survayinge, noe where stayinge;
Like unto the fierye elfe,
Over the topps of hyest mountaines skipping,
Over the plaines, the woods, the valleys, tripping.
Over the seas without oare of shipping,
Hollow, me fancy! wither wilt thou goe?

Amydst the cloudy vapors, faine wold I see
What are those burning tapors   10
Which benight us and affright us,
And what the meetors bee.
ffaine wold I know what is the roaring thunder,
And the bright lightning which cleeves the clouds in
    sunder,
And what the cometts are, att which men gaze and
    wonder.
Hollow, me, etc.

Looke but downe below me, where you may be bold,
Where none can see or know mee;
All the world of gadding, running of madding,
None can their stations hold: 20
One, he sitts drooping all in a dumpish passion;
Another, he is for mirth and recreation;
The third, he hangs his head because hees out of fassion.
Hollow, etc.

See, see, see, what a bustling!
Now I descry one another justlynge!
How they are turmoyling, one another foyling,
And how I past them bye!

Hee thats above, him thats below despiseth;
Hee thats below, doth envye him that ryseth;   30
Everye man his plot and counter plott deviseth.
Hollow, etc.

Shipps, shipps, shipps, I descry now!
Crossing the maine Ile goe too, and try now
What they are projecting and protecting;
And when they turne againe.
One, hees to keepe his country from invadinge;
Another, he is for merchandise and tradinge;
The other lyes att home like summers cattle shadding.
Hollow, etc.   40

Hollow, me fancy, hollow;
I pray thee come unto mee, I can noe longer follow!
I pray thee come and try *me*; doe not flye me!
Sithe itt will noe better bee,
Come, come away! Leave of thy lofty soringe!
Come stay att home, and on this booke be poring;
For he that gads abroad, he hath the lesse in storinge.
Welcome, my fancye! welcome home to mee!

ffinis

NEWARKE

Our braines are asleepe, then fyll us a cupp
  Of cappering sacke and clarett;
Here is a health to King Charles! then drinke it all up,
  His cause will fare better for itt.
Did not an ould Arke save Noye in a fflood?
  Why may not a new arke to us be us good?
Wee dread not their forces, they are all made of wood,
  Then wheele and turne about againe.

Though all beyond Trent be sold to the Scott,
  To men of a new protestation,   10
If Sandye come there, twill fall to their lott
  To have a new signed possession!
But if once Lesly gett *them* in his power,
  Gods Leard! heele play the devill and all!
But let him take heed how hee comes there,
  Lest Sweetelipps ring him a peale in his eare.

Then tosse itt up merrilye, fill to the brim!
  Wee have a new health to remember;
Heeres a health to our garrisons! drink it to them,
  Theyle keepe us all warme in December.   20
I care not a figg what enemy comes;
  For wee doe account them but hop-of-my-thumbes,
For Morrise our prince is coming amaine
  To rowte and make them run againe.

ffinis

AMONGST THE MIRTLES

Amongst the mirtles as I walket,
Love and my thoughts sights this inter-talket:
" Tell me," said I in deepe distresse,
" Where may I find *my sheperdesse?* "

" Thou foole! " said Love, " knowes thou not this?
In everye thing thats good shee is.
In yonder tulepe goe and seeke,
There thou may find her lipp, her cheeke;

" In yonder enameled pancye,
There thou shalt have her curyous eye;   1 0
In bloome of peach and rosee budd,
There wave the streamers of her blood;

" In brightest lyllyes that heere stand,
The emblemes of her whiter hands;
In yonder rising hill, their smells
Such sweet as in her bosome dwells."

" It is trew," said I; and thereupon
I went to plucke them one by one
To make of parts a unyon;
Butt on a sudden all was gone.   20

With that I stopt, sayd, " Love, these bee,
Fond man, resemblance-is of thee;
And as these flowers, thy joyes shall dye
Even in the twinkling of an eye,

" And all thy hopes of her shall wither
Like these short sweetes soe knitt together."

ffinis

THE WORLDE IS CHANGED

The world is changed, and wee have choyces,
Not by most reason, but most voyces;
The lyon is trampled by the mouse,
The Lower is the Upper House,
And thus from la[w]s orders come,
But now their orders [are] la[w]s frome.

In all humilitye they crave
Theire soveraigne to be their slave,
Beseeching him that hee wold bee
Betrayd to them most loyallye;   10
For it were meeknesse soe in him
To be a Vice-roy unto Pym.

If that hee wold but once lay downe
His scepter, majestye, and crowne,
Hee shalbe made in time to come
The greatest prince in Christendome.
Charles, att this time having noe neede,
Thankes them as much as if they did.

Petitions none must be presented
But what are by themselves invented,   20
That once a month they thinke it ffitting
To fast from s[in]ne because from sittinge;
Such blessings to the land are sent
By priviledge of Parlaiment.

ffinis

THE TRIBE OF BANBURYE

On the seventh day on the seventh month,
    Most lamentablye
The men of Babylon did spoyle
    The tribe of Banburye.

A brother post from Coventry
    Ryding in a blew rockett,
Sayes, " Colbronde Lunsford comes, I saw,
    With a childs arme hang in his pockett."

Then wee called up our men of warr,
    Younge Vivers, Cooke and Denys,   10
Whome our Lord Sea placed under
    His sonne Master ffyenys.

When hee came neere, he sent us word
    That hee was coming downe,
And wold, unles wee lett him in,
    Granado all our towne.

Then was our Colbronde—Fines—and me,
    In a most woefull case;
For neither he nor I did know
    Who this granado was.   20

Wee had eight gunnes called ordinance,
    And foure score musquetiers,
Yett all this wold not serve to stop
    Those Philistime Cavileeres.

Good people, they did send in men
    From Dorchester and Wickam;
But wher this gyant did them see,
    Good Lord, how he did kick han!

" You Round heads, rebells, rougs," quoth hee,
    " Ile crop and slitt eche eare,   30
And leave you neither arme nor lege
    Much longer then your heere!"

Then wee sett ope our gates full wyde;
    They swarmed in like bees,
And they were all arraydd in buffe
    Thicker then our towne cheese.

Now God deliver us, we pray,
    From such blood-thirstye men,
From Levyathan Lunsford
    Who eateth our children!   40

ffor Banburye, the tinkers crye,
    You hanged us up by twelves;
Now since Lunsford hath plundred you,
    You may goe hang your selves.

ffinis

AY ME: AY ME.

"Ay me, ay me, pore Sisley, and undone!
I had twelve sutors, now I have but one!
They all were wealthy; had I beene but wise;
Now have all left me since I have beene soe nice,
But only one, and him all maidens scorne,
For hees the worst, I thinke, that ere was borne."
"Peace, good Sisley! peace, and say noe more!
Bad mends in time; good salve heales many a sore."

"ffaith, such a one as I cold none but love,
For few or none of them doe constant prove;   10
A man in shape, proportion, looke, and showe,
Much like a mushroome in one night doth grow;
Proud as a jay thats of a comely hew,
Cladd like a musele in a capp of blew."
"Peace, good Sisley! peace, and say noe more!
Be merry, wench, and lett the welkin rore!"

"The first I had was framed in bewtyes mold,
The second, third, and fourth had store of gold,
The fifth, sixth, seventh, eighth had trades eche one,
The best had goods and lands to live upon;   20
Now may I weepe, sigh, sobb, and ring my hands,
Since this hath neither witt, trade, goods, nor lands."
"Peace, good Sisley; peace, and take that one
That stayes behind when all the rest are gone!"

"He *is*, as Turkes doe say, noe renegatoe,
Noe Portugall, Gallowne, or reformato;
But in playne termes some say he is a Scott,
That by his witts some old cast suite hath gott,

And now is as briske as my Bristow taylor,
And swaggers like a pander or a saylor."   30
" Kisse him, Sisley, kisse him, he may prove the best,
And use him kindly, but w[oe] bee all the rest."

" One was a Welchman, her wold scorne to crye ;
And three were Dutchmen that sill drunke wold bee ;
And six were Frenchemen that were pockye proude ;
And one a Spanyard that cold bragg alowd.
Now all are gone, and way not me a figge,
But one poore Scott who can doe nought but begg."
" Take him, Sisley ! take him, for itt is noe doubt,
His trades that beggs, heele never proofe banquerout." 40

" Nay, sure, Ile have him, for all people say
That men by begging grow rich now a day,
And that oftentimes is gotten with a word
Att great mens hands that never was woone by sword.
Then welcome, Scotchman, wee will weded bee,
And one day thou shalt begg for thee and mee."
" Well sayd, Sisley ! well said ! on another day,
By begging thou maist weare a garland gay ! "

FFAINE WOLDE I CHANGE

" Faine wold I change my maiden lifte
    To tast of loves true joyes."
" What? woldest thou chuse to bee a wiffe?
    Maids wishes are but toyes."
" How can there bee a greater hell
    Then live a maid soe long,
        a mayd soe long?
   " To the church; ring out the marriage bell,—
" Ding dong, ding dong, ding dong!"

" Beffore that fifteen yeeres were spent,
    I knew, and have a sonne."   10
" How old art thou?" " Sixteene next Lent."
   " Alas, wee are both undone!"
" How can there bee, etc."

" Besides, I heard an old wiffe tell
    That all true maids must dye."
" What must they doe?" " Lead apes in hell!
    A dolefull destinye.
" And wee will lead noe apes in hell;
    Weele change our maiden song,
        our maiden song;
" To the church; ring out the marriage bell,—   20
    Wee have lived true mayds to longe."

ffinis

WHEN FIRST I SAWE

When ffirst I saw [thee] I resolved
    To honor and renowne thee;
But if I be disdayned, I wishe
    That I had never knowne thee.
I asked leave; you bade me love;
    Is itt now time to chyde mee?
O no, no, no! I love you still, what fortune ever betyde
    mee!

If I admire or praise you too much,
    That [fault] *you* might forgive mee;
Or that my hand hath straid to touch,   10
    Thenn might you justly leave mee,
But I that liked, and you that loved,
    Is now a time to wrangle?
O no, no, no, my hart is ffixt, and will not new entangle.

The sun, whose beames most glorious are,
    Rejecteth noe beholder;
Your faire face, past all compare,
    Makes my faint hart the bolder.
When bewtye likes, and witt delights,
    And showes of love doe bind mee;   20
There, there! O there! whersoever I goe,
    Ile leave my hart behind mee!

ffinis

HOW FAYRE SHEE BE

Shall I, wasting in dispayre,
Dye because a womans fayre?
Or make pale my cheekes with care
Because anothers roseye are?
Be shee fairer then the day
Or the flowry meads in May,
If shee thinke not well of mee,
What care I how fayre shee bee?

Shall my foolish hart be pind
Because I see a woman kind,   10
Or a well disposed nature
With a comlye feature?
Be shee meeker, kinder, then
The turtledove or pelican,
If shee be not soe to me,
What care I how kind shee bee?

Shall a womans vertues move
Me to perish for her love,
Or her worthy merritts knowne
Make me quite forgett mine owne?   20
Were shee with that goodness blest,
As may meritt name of best,
If shee be not soe to me,
What care I how good shee bee?

Be shee good or kind or fayre,
I will never more dispair;
If shee love me, this beleeve,
I will dye ere she shall greive;
If shee slight me when I woe,
I will scorne and lett her goe.   30
Or if she bee not for mee,
What care I for whom shee bee?

COME, COME, COME!

Come, come, come! shall wee masque or mum?
    By my holly-d[om], what a coyle is heere!
Some must sway, and some obay,
    Or else, I pray, who stands in feare?
Though my toe, that I limpe on soe,
    Doe cause my woe and wellaway,
Yett this sweet spring and another thing
Will make you sing fa la la la la.

ffellow gods, will you fall att odds?
    What a fury madds your morttall braines!   10
For a litle care of the worlds affare,
    Will you frett, will you square, will you vexe
        you[r] vai[nes]?
No, gods! no! let fury go,
    And morttalls doe as well as they may!
For this sweet, etc.

God of moes, with thy toting nose,
    With thy mouth that growes to thy lolling eare,
Stretch thy mouth from north to south,
    And quench thy drought in vinigar!
Though thy toung be too large and too longe   20
    To sing this song of fa la la la la,
Joyne Momus grace to Vulcans pace,
    And with a filthy face crye " waw waw waw! "

Brother mine, thou art god of wine!
    Will you tast of the wine to the companye?
King of quaffe, carrouse and doffe
    Your liquor of, and follow mee!

Sweete soyle of Exus Ile,
  Wherin this coyle was every day,
For this sweet, etc.   30

Mercurye, thou Olimpian spye!
  Wilt thou wash thine eye in this fontaine cleere?
When you goe to the world below,
  You shall light of noe such liquor there,
Though you were a winged stare
  And flyeth farr as shineth day;
Yett heeres a thing your hart will wing,
  And make you sing, etc.

You that are the god of warr,
  A cruell starr perverse and froward,   40
Mars! prepare thy warlicke speare,
  And targett! heers a combatt toward!
Then fox me, and Ile fox thee;
  Then lets agree, and end this fray,
Since this sweet, etc.

Venus queene, for bewtye seene,
  In youth soe greene, and loved soe young,
Thou that art mine owne sweet hart,
  Shalt have a part in cuppe *and* songe;
Though my foot be wrong, my swords full long,   50
  And hart full strong; cast care away,
Since this sweet, etc.

Great Appollo, crowned with yellow,
  Cynthi[a]'s fellow, Muses' deere!
Heere is wine, itt must be thine,
  Itt will refine thy musicke cleere;
To the wire of this sweet lire,
  You must aspire another day,
For this sweet, etc.

Juno clere, and Mother dere,   60
        You come in the rere of a bowsing feast;
Thus I meet, your grace to greet;
        The grape is sweet and the last is best.
Now let fall your angry brawle
        From immortall and wayghtye sway;
Tis a gracious thing to please your King,
        And heare you sing, etc.

Awfull Sire, and King of fire!
        Let wine aspire to thy mighty throne,
And in this quire of voices clere   70
        Come thou, and beare an imorttall drame;
For fury ends, and grace desends
        With Stygian feinds to dwell for aye.
Lett nectur spring and thunder ring
        When Jove doth sing, etc.

Vulcan, Momus, Hermes, Bacchus,
        Mars and Venus, tooe and tooe,
Phebus brightest, Juno rightest,
        And the mightyest of the crew,
Jove, and all the heavens great hall,   80
        Keepe festivall and holy-day!
Since this sweete spring with her blacke thing
        Will make you sing fa la la la.

                        ffinis.

THE GRENE KNIGHT

List! wen Arthur he was King,
He had all att his leadinge
    The broad Ile of Brittaine;
England and Scottland one was,
And Wales stood in the same case,
    The truth itt is not to layne.

He drive allyance out of this Ile,
Soe Arthur lived in peace a while,
    As men of mickle maine,
Knights strong of their degree   10
Strove which of them hyest shold bee;
    Therof Arthur was not faine;

Hee made the Round Table for their behove,
That none of them shold sitt above,
    But all shold sitt as one,
The King himselfe in state royall,
Dame Guenever our Queene withall,
    Seemlye of body and bone.

Itt fell againe the Christmase,
Many came to that Lords place,   20
    To that worthye one
With helme on head, and brand bright,
All that tooke order of knight;
    None wold linger att home.

There was noe castle nor manour free
That might harbour that companye,
    Their puissance was soe great.

Their tents up they pight
For to lodge there all that night,
    Therto were sett to meate.   30

Messengers there came *and* went
With much victualls verament
    Both by way and streete;
Wine and wild fowle thither was brought,
Within they spared nought
    For gold, and they might itt gett.

Now of King Arthur noe more I mell;
But of a venterous knight I will you tell
    That dwelled in the west countrye;
Sir Bredbeddle, for sooth he hett;   40
He was a man of mickele might,
    And lord of great bewtye.

He had a lady to his wiffe,
He loved her deerlye as his liffe,
    Shee was both blyth and blee;
Because Sir Gawaine was stiffe in stowre,
Shee loved him privilye paramour,
    And shee never him see.

Itt was Agostes that was her mother;
Itt was witchcraft and noe other   50
    That shee dealt with all;

Shee cold transpose knights and swaine
Like as in battaile they were slaine,
    Wounded both lim and lightt,
Shee taught her sonne the knight alsoe
In transposed likenesse he shold goe
    Both by fell and frythe;

R   121

Shee said, " Thou shalt to Arthurs hall;
For there great adventures shall befall
    That ever saw king or knight."   60
All was for her daughters sake,
That which she soe sadlye spake
    To her sonne-in-law the knight,
Because Sir Gawaine was bold and hardye,
And therto full of curtesye,
    To bring him into her sight.

The knight said " Soe mote I thee,
To Arthurs court will I mee hye
    For to praise thee right,
And to prove Gawaines points three;   70
And that be true that men tell me,
    By Mary most of might."

Earlye, soone as itt was day,
The knight dressed him full gay,
    Umstrode a full good steede;
Helm and hawberke both he hent,
A long fauchion verament
    To fend them in his neede.

That was a jolly sight to seene,
When horsse and armour was all greene,   80
    And weapon that hee bare.
When that burne was harnisht still,
His countenance he became right well,
    I dare itt safelye sweare.

That time att Carleile lay our King;
Att a castle of Flatting was his dwelling,
    In the fforrest of Delamore.
For sooth he rode, the sooth to say,
To Carleile he came on Christmas Day,
    Into that fayre countrye.   90

When he into that place came,
The porter thought him a marvelous groome :
  He saith, " Sir, wither wold yee ? "
Hee said, " I am a venterous knight,
And of your King wold have sight,
  And other lords that heere bee."

Noe word to him the porter spake,
But left him standing att the gate,
  And went forth, as I weene,
And kneeled downe before the King ;   100
Saith, " In lifes dayes old or younge,
  Such a sight I have not seene !

" For yonder, att your gates right,"
He saith, " hee is a venterous knight;
  All his vesture is greene."
Then spake the King proudest in all,
Saith, " Bring him into the hall ;
  Let us see what hee doth meane."

When the greene knight came before the King,
He stood in his stirrops strechinge,   110
  And spoke with voice cleere,
And saith, " King Arthur, God save thee,
As thou sittest in thy prosperitye,
  And maintaine thine honor !

" Why thou wold me nothing but right ;
I am come hither a venterous *knight*,
  And kayred thorrow countrye farr,
To prove poynts in thy pallace
That longeth to manhood in everye case
  Among thy lords deere."   120

The King, he sayd full still
Till he had said all his will;
 Certein thus can he say:
"As I am true knight and King,
Thou shalt have thy askinge!
 I will not say th[ee] nay,

"Whether thou wilt on foote fighting,
Or on steed backe justing
 For love of ladyes gay.
If and thine armor be not fine,   130
I will give thee part of mine."
 "God amercy, Lord!" can he say,

"Here I make a challenging
Among the lords both old and younge
 That worthy beene in weede,
Which of them will take in hand—
Hee that is both stiffe and stronge
 And full good att need—

"I shall lay my head downe,
Strike itt of if he can,   140
 With a stroke to garr itt bleed,
For this day twelve monthe another at his:
Let me see who will answer this,
 A knight that is doughtye of deed;

"For this day twelve month, the sooth to say,
Let him come to me and seicth his praye,
 Rudlye, or ever hee blin;
Whither to come, I shall him tell,
The readie way to the greene chappell,
 That place I will be in."   150

The King att ease sate full still,
And all his lords said but litle
     Till he had said all his will.
Upp stood Sir Kay, that crabbed knight,
Spake mightye words that were of height,
     That were both loud and shrill;

" I shall strike his necke in tooe,
The head away the body froe."
     They bade him all be still,
Saith, " Kay, of thy dints make noe rouse,   160
Thou wottest full litle what thou does;
     Noe good, but mickle ill."

Eche man wold this deed have done.
Up start Sir Gawaine soone,
     Upon his knees can kneele,
He said, " That were great villanye
Without you put this deede to me,
     My leege, as I have s[eele];

" Remember, I am your sisters sonne."
The King said, " I grant thy boone;   170
     But mirth is best att meele;
Cheere thy guest, and give him wine,
And after dinner, to itt fine,
     And sett the buffett well! "

Now the greene knight is set att meate,
Seemlye served in his seate,
     Beside the Round Table.
To talke of his welfare, nothing he needs,
Like a knight himselfe he feeds,
     With long time reasnable.   180

When the dinner, it was done,
The King said to Sir Gawaine soone,
    Withouten any fable
He said, " On you will doe this deede,
I pray Jesus be your speede!
    This knight is nothing unstable."

The greene knight his head downe layd;
Sir Gawaine, to the axe he braid
    To strike with eger will;
He stroke the necke bone in twaine,   190
The blood burst out in everye vaine,
    The head from the body fell.

The greene knight his head up hent,
Into his saddle wightilye he sprent,
    Spake words both lowd and shrill,
Saith: " Gawaine! thinke on thy covenant!
This day twelve monthes see thou ne want
    To come to the greene chappell!"

All had great marvell, that they see
That he spake so merrilye,   200
    And bare his head in his hand.
Forth att the hall dore he rode right,
And that saw both King and knight
    And lords that were in land.

Without the hall dore, the sooth to saine,
Hee sett his head upon againe,
    Saies, " Arthur, have heere my hand!
When-soever the knight cometh to mee,
A better buffett sickerlye
    I dare him well warrand."   210

The greene knight away went.
All this was done by enchantment
    That the old witch had wrought.
Sore sicke fell Arthur the King,
And for him made great mourning
    That into such bale was brought.

The Queen, shee weeped for his sake;
Sorry was Sir Lancelott Dulake,
    And other were dreery in thought
Because he was brought into great perill;   220
His mightye manhood will not availe,
    That before hath freshlye fought.

Sir Gawaine comfort King and Queen,
And all the doughtye there be-deene;
    He bade they shold be still;
Said, "Of my deede I was never feard,
Nor yett I am nothing a-dread,
    I swere by Saint Michaell;

"For when draweth toward my day,
I will dresse me in mine array   230
    My promise to fulfill.
Sir," he saith, "as I have blis,
I wott not where the greene chappell is,
    Therfore seeke itt I will."

The royall cou[r]tt verament
All rought Sir Gawaines intent,
    They thought itt was the best.
They went forth into the feild,
Knights that ware both speare and sheeld
    They priced forth full prest;   240

127

Some chuse them to justinge,
Some to dance, revell, and sing;
    Of mirth they wold not rest.
All they swore together in fere,
That and Sir Gawaine over-come were,
    They wold bren all the west.

Now leave wee the King in his pallace.
The greene knight come home is
    To his owne castle;
This folke frend when he came home   250
What doughtye deeds he had done.
    Nothing he wold them tell;

Full well hee wist in certaine
That his wiffe loved Sir Gawaine
    That comelye was under kell.
Listen, lords! and yee will sitt,
And yee shall heere the second ffitt,
    What adventures Sir Gawaine befell.

Second Parte

The day is come that Gawaine must gone;
Knights and ladyes waxed wann   260
    That were without in that place;
The King himselfe siked ill,
Ther Queen a swounding almost fell
    To that jorney when he shold passe.

When he was in armour bright,
He was one of the goodlyest knights
    That ever in Brittaine was borne.
They brought Sir Gawaine a steed,
Was dapple gray and good att need,
    I tell withouten scorne;   270

His bridle was with stones sett,
With gold and pearle overfrett,
    And stones of great vertue;
He was of a furley kind;
His stirropps were of silke of Ynd;
    I tell you this tale for true.

When he rode over the mold,
His geere glistered as gold.
    By the way as he rode,
Many furleys he there did see,   280
Fowles by the water did flee,
    By brimes and bankes soe broad.

Many furleys there saw hee
Of wolves and wild beasts sikerlye;
    On hunting hee tooke most heede.
Forth he rode, the sooth to tell,
For to seeke the greene chappell,
    He wist not where indeed.

As he rode in an evening late,
Riding downe a greene gate,   290
    A faire castell saw hee,
That seemed a place of mickle pride;
Thitherward Sir Gawaine can ryde
    To gett some harborrowe.

Thither he came in the twylight,
He was ware of a gentle knight,
    The lord of the place was hee.
Meekly to him Sir Gawaine can speake,
And asked him, " For King Arthurs sake,
    Of harborrowe I pray thee!   300

"I am a far labordd knight,
I pray you lodge me all this night."
        He sayd him not nay,
Hee tooke him by the arme and led him to the hall.
A poore child can hee call,
        Saith, "Dight well this palfrey."

Into a chamber they went a full great speed;
There they found all things readye att need,
        I dare safelye swere;
Fier in chambers burning bright,   310
Candles in chandlers burning light;
        To supper they went full yare.

He sent after his ladye bright
To come to supp with that gentle knight,
        And shee came blythe with-all;
Forth shee came then anon,
Her maids following her eche one
        In robes of rich pall.

As shee sate att her supper,
Ever-more the ladye clere   320
        Sir Gawaine shee looked upon.
When the supper it was done,
She tooke her maids, and to her chamber gone.

He cheered the knight and gave him wine,
And said "Welcome, by St. Martine!
        I pray you take itt for none ill;
One thing, Sir, I wold you pray;
What you make soe farr this way?
        The truth you wold me tell;

"I am a knight, and soe are yee;   330
Your concell, an you will tell mee,
      Forsooth keepe itt I will;
For if itt be poynt of any dread,
Perchance I may helpe att need
      Either lowd or still."

For his words that were soe smooth
Had Sir Gawaine wist the soothe,
      All he wold not have told,
For that was the greene knight
That hee was lodged with that night,   340
      And harbarrowes in his hold.

He saith, "As to the greene chappell,
Thitherward I can you tell,
      Itt is but furlongs three.
The master of it is a venterous knight,
And workes by witchcraft day and night,
      With many a great furley.

"If he worke with never soe much frauce,
He is curteous as he sees cause.
      I tell you sikerlye,   350
You shall abyde, and take your rest,
And I will into yonder fforrest
      Under the greenwood tree."

They plight their truthes to beleeve,
Either with other for to deale,
      Whether it were silver or gold;
He said, "We two both *sworn* wilbe,
Whatsoever God sends you and mee,
      To be parted on the mold."

The greene knight went on hunting;   360
Sir Gawaine in the castle beinge,
    Lay sleeping in his bed.
Uprose the old witche with hast throwe,
And to her dauhter can shee goe,
    And said " Be not adread!"

To her daughter can shee say,
" The man that thou hast wisht many a day,
    Of him thou maist be sped;
For Sir Gawaine, that curteous knight,
Is lodged in this hall all night."   370
    Shee brought her to his bedd.

Shee saith, " Gentle knight, awake!
And for this faire ladies sake
    That hath loved thee soe deere,
Take her boldly in thine armes,
There is noe man shall doe thee harme;"
    Now beene they both heere.

The ladye kissed him times three,
Saith, " Without I have the love of thee,
    My life standeth in dere."   380
Sir Gawaine blushed on the lady bright,
Saith, " Your husband is a gentle knight,
    By Him that bought mee deare!

" To me itt were great shame
If I shold doe him any grame,
    That hath beene kind to mee;
For I have such a deede to doe,
That I can neyther rest nor roe,
    Att an end till itt bee."

Then spake that ladye gay, 390
Saith, " Tell me some of your journey,
   Your succour I may bee;
If itt be poynt of any warr,
There shall noe man doe you noe darr,
   And yee wilbe governed by mee;

" For heere I have a lace of silke,
It is as white as any milke,
   And of a great value."
Shee saith, " I dare safelye sweare
There shall noe man doe you deere 400
   When you have it upon you."

Sir Gawaine spake mildlye in the place,
He thanked the lady and tooke the lace,
   And promised her to come againe.
The knight in the fforrest slew many a hind,
Other venison he cold none find
   But wild bores on the plaine.

Plentye of does and wild swine,
Foxes and other ravine,
   As I hard true men tell. 410
Sir Gawaine swore sickerlye
" Home to your owne, welcome you bee,
   By Him that harrowes hell!"

The greene knight his venison downe layd;
Then to Sir Gawaine thus hee said,
   " Tell me anon in heght,
What noveltyes that you have won,
For heers plenty of venison."
   Sir Gawaine said full right,

Sir Gawaine sware by St. Leonard,   420
" Such as God sends, you shall have part : "
  In his armes he hent the knight,
And there he kissed him times three,
Saith, " Heere is such as God sends mee,
  By Mary most of might."

Ever privilye he held the lace :
That was all the villanye that ever was
  Prooved by Sir Gawaine the gay.
Then to bed soone they went,
And sleeped there verament   430
  Till morrow itt was day.

Then Sir Gawaine, soe curteous and free,
His leave soone taketh hee
  Att the lady soe gaye ;
Hee thanked her, and tooke the lace,
And rode towards the chappell apace ;
  He knew noe whitt the way.

Ever more in his thought he had
Whether he shold worke as the ladye bade,
  That was soe curteous and sheene.   440
The greene knight rode another way ;
He transposed him in another array,
  Before as it was greene.

As Sir Gawaine rode over the plaine,
He hard one high upon a mountaine
  A horne blowne full lowde.
He looked after the greene chappell,
He saw itt stand under a hill
  Covered with euyes about ;

He looked after the greene knight,   450
He hard him wehett a fauchion bright,
    That the hills rang about.
The knight spake with strong cheere,
Said, "Yee be welcome, Sir Gawaine heere,
    It behooveth thee to lowte."
He stroke, and litle perced the skin,
Unneth the flesh within.
    Then Sir Gawaine had noe doubt;

He saith, "Thou shontest! why dost thou soe?"
Then Sir Gawaine in hart waxed throe;   460
    Upon his ffeete can stand,
And soone he drew out his sword,
And saith, "Traitor! if thou speake a word,
    Thy liffe is in my hand;
I had but one stroke att thee,
And thou hast had another att mee,
    Noe falshood in me thou found!"

The knight said withouten laine,
"I wend I had Sir Gawaine slaine,
    The gentlest knight in this land;   470
Men told me of great renowne,
Of curtesie thou might have woon the crowne
    Above both free and bound,

"And alsoe of great gentrye;
And now three points be put fro thee,
    It is the moe pittye:
Sir Gawaine! thou wast not leele
When thou didst the lace conceale
    That my wiffe gave to thee!

"ffor wee were both, thou wist full well,   480
For thou hadst the halfe dale
        Of my venerye;
If the lace had never beene wrought,
To have slaine thee was never my thought,
        I swere by God verelye!

"I wist it well my wiffe loved thee;
Thou wold doe me noe villanye,
        But nicked her with nay;
But wilt thou doe as I bidd thee,
Take me to Arthurs court with thee,   490
        Then were all to my pay."

Now are the knights accorded thore;
To the castle of Hutton can they fare,
        To lodge there all that night.
Earlye on the other day
To Arthurs court they tooke the way
        With harts blyth and light.

All the court was full faine,
Alive when they saw Sir Gawaine;
        They thanked God abone.   500
That is the matter and the case
Why Knights of the Bathe weare the lace
        Untill they have wonen their shoen,

Or else a ladye of hye estate
From about his necke shall it take,
        For the doughtye deeds that hee hath done.
It was confirmed by Arthur the King;
Thorrow Sir Gawaines desiringe
        The King granted him his boone.

Thus endeth the tale of the greene knight. 510
God, that is soe full of might,
    To heaven their soules bring
That have hard this litle storye
That fell some times in the west countrye
    In Arthurs days our King!

ffinis

SIR TRIAMORE

Lo[rd] Jesus Christ, o[f] heaven King,
Grant you all his deare blessing,
    And his heaven for to win!
If you will a stond lay to your eare,
Of adventures you shall heare
    That wilbe to your liking,

Of a King and of a Queene,
That had great joy them betweene;
    Sir Arradas was his name;
He had a Queene named Margarett,   10
Shee was as true as steele, and sweet,
    And full false brought in fame

By the Kings steward that Marrocke hight,
A traitor and a false knight:
    Herafter yee will say all the same.
Hee looved well that ladye gent;
And for shee wold not with him consent,
    He did that good Queene much shame.

This King loved well his Queene
Because shee was comlye to be seene,   20
    And as true as the turtle on tree.
Either to other made great moane,
For children together had they none
    Begotten on their bodye;

Therfore the King, I understand,
Made a vow to goe to the Holy Land,
    There for to fight and for to slay;
And praid God that He wold send him tho
Grace to gett a child be-tweene them tow,
    That the right heire might bee.   30

For his vow he did there make,
And of the Pope the Crosse he did take,
    For to seek the land were God him bought.
The night of his departing, on the ladye mild,
As God it wold, hee gott a child;
    But they both wist itt naught.

And on the morrow when it was day
The King hyed on his journey;
    For to tarry, he it not thought.
Then the Queene began to mourne   40
Because her lord wold noe longer sojourne;
    Shee sighed full sore, and sobbed oft.

The King and his men armed them right,
Both lords, barrons, and many a knight,
    With him for to goe.
Then betweene her and the King
Was much sorrow and mourninge
    When they shold depart in too.

He kissed and tooke his leave of the Queene,
And other ladies bright and sheene,   50
    And of Marrocke his steward alsoe;
The King commanded him on paine of his life
For to keepe well his Queene and wiffe
    Both in weale and woe.

Now is the King forth gone
To the place where God was on the Crosse done,
    And warreth there a while.
Then bethought this false steward—
As yee shall here after*ward*,—
    His lord and King to beguile;   60

He wooed the Queene day and night
For to lye with her, and he might;
    He dread no creature thoe.
ffull fayre hee did that lady speake,
That he might in bed with that ladye sleepe;
    Thus full oft he prayed her thoe.

But shee was stedfast in her thought,
And heard [him] speake, and said nought
    Till hee all his case had told.
Then shee said, "Marrocke, hast thou not thought,   70
All that thou speakeest is ffor nought?
    I trow not that thou wold;

" For well my lord did trust thee,
When hee to you delivered mee
    To have me under the hold;
And *thou* woldest full faine
To doe thy lord shame!
    Traitor, thou art to bold!"

Then said Marrocke unto that ladye,
" My lord is gone now verelye   80
    Against Gods foes for to ffight;
And, without the more wonder bee,
Hee shall come noe more att thee,
    As I am a true knight.

" And Madam, wee will worke soe privilye,
That wethere he doe live or dye,
    For of this shall witt noe wyght."
Then waxed the Queene wonderous *wroth*,
And swore many a great othe
    As shee was a true woman,   90

Shee said, " Traitor! if ever thou be soe hardiye
To show me of such villanye,
    On a gallow tree I will thee hange!
If I may know after this
That thou tice me, I-wis,
    Thou shalt have the law of the land."

Sir Marroccke said, " Ladye, mercye!
I said itt for noe villainey,
    By Jesu, heaven Kinge!
But only for to prove your will,   100
Whether that you were good or ill,
    And for noe other thinge;

" But now, Madam, I may well see,
You are as true as turtle on the tree
    Unto my lord the King;
And itt is to me both glad and leefe;
Therfore take it not into greefe
    For noe manner of thinge."

And soe the traitor excused him thoe,
The lady wend itt had beene soe   110
    As the steward had said.
He went forth, and held him still,
And thought he cold not have his will;
    Therfore hee was evill apayd.

Soe with treason and trecherye
He thought to doe her villanye;
    Thus to himselfe he said.
Night and day hee laboured then
For to betray that good woman;
    Soe att the last he her betraid.   120

Now of this good Queene leave wee,
And by the grace of the Holy Trinitye
    Full great with child did shee gone.
Now of King Arradas speake wee,
That soe farr in heathinnesse is hee
    To fight against Gods fone;

There with his army and all his might
Slew many a Sarrazen in fight.
    Great words of them there rose
In the heathen land, and alsoe in Pagainey;   130
And in everye other land that they come bye,
    There sprang of him great losse.

When *he* had done his pilgrimage,
And labored all that great voyage
    With all his good will and lybertye,—
Att fflome Jorden and att Bethlem,
And att Calvarye beside Jerusalem,
    In all the places was hee;—

Then he longed to come home
To see his ladye that lived at one;   140
    He thought ever on her greatlye.
Soe long they sealed on the fome
Till att the last they came home;
    He arrived over the [salte] strond.

The shippes did strike their sayles eche one,
The men were glad the King came home
    Unto his owne land.
There was both mirth and game,
The Queene of his cominge was glad and faine,
    Eche of them told other tydand.   150

The King at last his Queene beheld,
And saw heer goe great with childe:
    And hee wondred att that thinge.
Many a time he did her kisse,
And made great joy without misse;
    His hart made great rejoceinge.

Soone after the King hard tydinges newe
By Marroccke: that false knight untrue
    With reason his lord gan fraine,
"My lord," he sayd, "for Gods [p]yne!   160
For of that childe that never was thine,
    Why art thow soe fayne?

"You wend that itt your owne bee;
But," he said, "Sir, ffor certaintye
    Your Queene hath you betraine;
Another knight, soe God me speed,
Begott this child sith you yeed,
    And hath thy Queene forlaine."

"Alas!" said the King, "how may this bee?
For I betooke her unto thee,   170
    Her to keepe in waile and woe;
And under thy keeping how fortuned this
That thou suffered her doe amisse?
    Alas, Marroccke! why did thou soe?"
"Sir," said the steward, "blame not me;
For much mone shee made for thee,
    As though shee had loved noe moe;

143

"I trowed on her noe villanye
Till I saw one lye her by,
        As the mele had wrought.   180
To him I came with egar mood,
And slew the traitor as he stood;
        Full sore itt *me* forethought.

"Then shee trowed shee shold be shent,
And promised me both land and rent;
        Soe fayre shee me besought
To doe with her all my will
If that I wold *keepe* me still,
        And tell you naught."

"Of this," said the King, "I have great wonder;   190
For sorrow my hart will breake assunder!
        Why hath shee done amisse?
Alas! to whome shall I me mone,
Sith I have lost my comlye Queene
        That I was wont to kisse?"

The King said, "Marroccke, what is thy read?
It is best to turne to dead
        My Ladye that hath done me this;
Now because that shee is false to mee,
I will never more her see,   200
        Nor deale with her, I-wisse."

The steward said, "Lord, doe not soe;
Thou shalt neither burne ne sloe,
        But doe as I you shall you tell."
Marroccke sayd, "This councell I:
Banish her out of your land privilye,
        Far into exile.

" Deliver her an ambling steede,
And an old knight to her lead;
   Thus by my councell see yee doe;   210
And give them some money [for] spending
That may them out of the land bring;
   I wold noe better then soe.

" And an other mans child shalbe you[r] heyre,
Itt were neither good nor fayre
   But if itt were of your kin."
Then said the King, " Soe mote I thee,
Right as thou sayest, soe shall it bee,
   And erst will I never blin."

Loe, now is exiled that good Queene;   220
But shee wist not what it did meane,
   Nor what made him to begin.
To speake to her he nay wold;
That made the Queenes hart full cold,
   And that was great pittye and sin.

He did her cloth in purple weede,
And set her on an old steed
   That was both crooked and almost blinde;
He tooke her an old knight,
Kine to the Queene, Sir Rodger hight,   230
   That was both curteous and kind.

Three dayes he gave them leave to passe,
And after that day sett was,
   If men might them find,
The Queene shold burned be starke dead
In a ffyer with flames redd :
   This came of the stewards mind.

Forty florences for their expence
The King did give them in his presence,
    And commanded them to goe.   240
The Ladye mourned as shee shold dye;
For all this shee wist not whye
    Hee fared with her soe.

That good knight comforted the Queene,
And said, " Att Gods will all must beene;
    Therfore, Madam, mourne you noe more."
Sir Rodger for her hath much care,
For ofte she mourned as she dyd fare,
    And cryed and sighed full sore;

Lords, knights, and ladyes gent   250
Mourned for her when shee went,
    And be-wayled her that season.
The Queene began to make sorrow and care
When shee from the King shold fare
    With wrong, against all reason.
Forth they went, in number three,
Sir Rodger, the Queene, and his greyhound Trulye;
    Ah! [w]o worth wicked treason!

Then thought the steward trulye
To doe the Queene a villanye,   260
    And to worke with her his will.
He ordained him a companye
Of his owne men privilye
    That wold assent him till;

All under a wood side they did lye
Wheras the Queene shold passe by,
    And held them wonderous still;
And there he thought verelye
His good Queene for to lye by,
    His lusts for to fulfill.   270

146

And when [they] came into the wood,
Sir Rodger and the Queene soe good,
    And there to passe with-out doubt;
With that they were ware of the steward,
How hee was coming to them ward
    With a ffull great rout.

"Heere is treason!" then said the Queene.
"Alas!" said Roger, "what may this meane?
    With foes wee be sett round about."
The knight sayd, "Heere will wee dwell;   280
Our liffe wee shall full deere sell,
    Be they never soe stout.

"Madam," he sayd, "be not affrayd,
For I thinke heere with this sword
    That I shall make them lowte."
Then cryed the steward to Sir Rodger on hye,
And said, "Lord, traitor! thou shalt dye!
    For that I goe about."

Sir Roger said, "Not for thee!
My death shalt thou deare abye;   290
    For with thee will I fight."
He went to him shortlye,
And old Sir Rodger bare him manfullye
    Like a full hardye knight;

He hewed on them boldlye;
There was none of that companye
    Soe hardye nor sow wight.
Sir Rodger hitt one on the head
That to the girdle the sword yeed,
    Then was hee of them quitte;   300

He smote a stroke with a sword good,
That all about them ran the blood,
    Soe sore he did them smite;
Trulye-hee, his greyhound that was soo good,
Did helpe his master, and by him stood,
    And bitterlye can hee byte.

Then that Lady, that fayre foode,
She feared Marrocke in her mood;
    Shee light on foote, and left her steede,
And ran fast, and wold not leave,   310
And hid her under a greene greave,
    For shee was in great dread.

Sir Rodger then the Queene can behold,
And of his liffe he did nothing hold;
    His good grayhound did help him indeed,
And, as itt is in the Romans told,
Fourteen he slew of yeomen bold;
    Soe he quitted him in that steade.

If hee had beene armed, I-wisse,
All the masterye had been his;   320
    Alas, hee lacked weed.
As good Sir Rodger gave a stroake,
Behind him came Sir Marroccke,—
    That evill might he speed,—

He smote Sir Rodger with a speare,
And to the ground he did him beare,
    And fast that knight did bleed.
Sir Marroccke gave him such a wound
That he dyed there on ground,
    And that was a sinfull deede.   330

Now is Rodger slaine certainlye.
He rode forth and let him lye,
    And sought after the Queene.
Fast hee rode, and sought everye way,
Yet wist he not where the Queene laye.
    Then [had] the traitor teene;

Over all the wood hee her sought;
But as God wold, he found her nought.
    Then waxed he wrath, I weene,
And held his journey evill besett,   340
That with the Queene had not mett
    To have had his pleasure, the traitor keene.

And when he cold not the Lady finde,
Homeward they began to wend,
    Hard by where Sir Rodger lay.
The steward him thrust throughout,
For of his death he had noe doubt,
    And this the Storye doth say.

And when the traitor had done soe,
He let him lye and went him froe,   350
    And tooke noe thought that day;
Yett all his companye was nye gone,
Fourteen he left there dead for one;
    There passed but four away.

Then the Queene was ffull woe,
And shee saw that they were goe,
    Shee made sorrow and crye.
Then shee rose and went againe
To Sir Rodger, and found him slaine;
    His grey-hound by his feet did lye.   360

"Alas," shee said, " that I was borne !
My trew knight that I have lorne,
    They have him there slaine ! "
Full pitteouslye shee mad her moane,
And said, " Now must I goe alone ! "
    The grey-hound shee wold have had full faine ;

The hound still by his master did lye,
He licked his wounds, and did whine and crye.
    This to see the Queene had paine,
And said, " Sir Roger, this hast thou for me !   370
Alas that *it* shold ever bee ! "
    Her hayre shee tare in twayne ;

And then shee went and tooke her steed,
And wold noe longer there abyde
    Lest men shold find her there.
Shee said, " Sir Roger, now thou art dead,
Who will the right way now me lead ?
    For now thow mayst speake noe more."

Right on the ground there as he lay dead,
Shee kist him or shee from him yead.   380
    God wott, her hart was sore !
What for sorrow and dread,
Fast away shee can her speede,
    Shee wist not wither nor where.

The good grayhound, for waile and woe,
From the knight hee wold not goe,
    But lay and licked his wound ;
He waite to have healed them againe,
And therto he did his paine :
    Loe, such love is in a hound !   390

This knight lay till he did stinke;
The greayhound he began to thinke,
    And scraped a pitt anon;
Therin he drew the dead corse,
And covered itt with earth and mosse,
    And from him he wold not gone.

The grayhound lay still there;
This Queene gan forth to fare
    For dread of her fone;
Shee had great sorrow in her hart,   400
The thornes pricked her wonderous smart,
    Shee wist not wither to goe.

This Lady forth fast can hye
Into the land of Hu[n]garye;
    Thither came shee with great woe.
At last shee came to a wood side,
But then cold shee noe further ryde,
    Her paynes tooke her soe.

Shee lighted downe in that tyde,
For there shee did her trau[ve]ell abyde;   410
    God wold that it shold be soe.
Then shee with much paine
Tyed her horsse by the rayne,
    And rested her there till her paynes were goe.

Shee was delivered of a manchild sweete;
And when it began to crye and weepe,
    It joyed her hart greatlye.
Soone after, when shee might stirr,
Shee tooke her child to her full neere,
    And wrapt itt full softlye.   420

What for wearye and for woe,
They fell a-sleepe both towe;
    Her steed stood her behind.
Then came a knight rydand there,
And found this Ladye soe lovelye of cheere
    As hee hunted after the hind.

The knight hight Bernard Mowswinge,
That found the Queene sleepinge,
    Under the greenwoode lyande.
Softlye he went neere and neere;   430
He went on foot, and beheld her cheere,
    As a knight curteous and kind.

He awaked that Ladye of beawtye;
Shee looked on him pitteouslee,
    And was affrayd full sore.
He said, " What doe you here, Madame?
Of whence be you, or whats your name?
    Have you your men forlorne? "

" Sir," shee sayd, " if you will witt,
My name is called Margerett;   440
    In Arragon I was borne;
Heere I sufferd much greefe;
Helpe me, sir, out of this mischeefe!
    Att some towne that I were."

The knight beheld the Ladye good;
Hee thought shee was of gentle blood
    That was soe hard bestead;
He tooke her up curteouslye,
And the child that lay her bye;
    Them both with him he led,   450

And made her have a woman att will,
Tendinge of her, as itt was skill,
    All for to bring her a-bedd.
Whatsoever shee wold have,
Shee needed itt not long to crave,
    Her speech was right soone sped.

They christened the child with great honour,
And named him Sir Tryamore.
    Then they were of him glad;
Great gifts to him was given   460
Of lords and ladyes by-deene,
    In bookes as I read.

There dwelled that Ladye longe
With much joy them amonge;
    Of her they were never wearye.
The child was taught great nurterye;
A master had him under his care,
    And taught him curtesie.
This child waxed wonderous well,
Of great stature both of fleshe and fell;   470
    Every man loved him trulye,

Of his companye all folke were glad:
Indeed, noe other cause they had,
    The child was gentle and bold.
Now of the Queene let wee bee,
And of the grayhound speake wee
    That I erst of told.

Long seven yeeres, soe God me save,
He did keepe his master's grave,
    Till that hee waxed old;   480
This grayhound Sir Roger kept long,
And brought him up sith he was younge,
    In Story as it is told;

Therfore he kept soe there,
For the space of seven yeere,
    And goe from him he ne wold.
Ever upon his masters grave he lay,
There might noe man have him away
    For heat neither for cold,

Without it were once a day   490
He ran about to gett his prey
    Of beasts that were bold,
Conyes, when he can them gett;
Thus wold he labor for his meate,
    Yett great hungar he had in how.

And seven yeeres he dwelled there,
Till itt beffell on that yeere,
    Even on Christmasse Day,
The gray-hound (as the Story sayes)
Came to the Kings palace   500
    Without any delay.
When they lords were sett at meate, soone
The grayhound into the hall runn
    Amonge the knights gay;

All about he can behold,
But he see not what hee wold;
    Then went he his way full right
When he had sought and cold not find;
ffull gentlye he did his kind,
    Speed better when he might.   510

The grayhound ran forth his way
Till he came where his master lay,
    As fast as ever he mought.
The King marveiled at that deed,
From whence he went, and whither he yeed,
    Or who him thither brought.

The King thought he had seene him ere,
But he wist not well where,
    Therfor he said right nought.
Soone he bethought him then   520
That he did him erst ken,
    And still stayd in that thought.

The other day, in the same wise,
When the King shold from his meate rise,
    The grayhound came in thoe;
All about there he sought,
But the steward found he nought;
    Then againe he began to goe.

Then sayd the King in that stond,
" Methinkes it is Sir Rogers hound   530
    That went forth with the Queene;
I trow they be come againe to this land.
Lords, all this I understand,
    It may right well soe bee[ne];

" If that they be into this land come,
We shall have word therof soone
    And within short space;
For never since they went, I-wisse,
I saw not the gray hound ere this;
    It is a marveilous case!   540

" When he cometh againe, follow him,
For evermore he will run
    To his masters dwelling place;
Run and goe, looke ye not spare,
Till that yee come there
    To Sir Rodger and my Queene."

Then the third day, amonge them all
The grayhound came into the hall,
　　To meate ere they were sett.
Marrocke the steward was within,　　　　　　550
The grayhound thought he wold not blin
　　Till he with him had mett;

He tooke the steward by the throte,
And assunder he it bote;
　　But then he wold not byde,
For to his grave he rann.
There followed him many a man,
　　Some on horsse, some beside;

And when he came where his master was,
He layd him downe beside the grasse　　　　560
　　And barked at the men againe.
There might noe man him from the place gett,
And yett with staves they did him beate,
　　That he was almost slaine.

And when the men saw noe better boote,
Then the men yeed home on horsse and foote,
　　With great wonder, I weene.
The King said, " By Gods paine,
I trow Sir Marrocke hath Sir Rodger slaine,
　　And with treason famed my Queene.　　　570

" Goe yee and seeke there againe;
For the hounds master there is slaine,
　　Some treason there hath beene."
Thither they went, soe God me save,
And found Sir Roger in his grave,
　　For that was soone seene:

156

And there they looked him there upon,
For he was hole both flesh and bone,
    And to the court his body they brought.
For when the King did him see, 580
The teares ran downe from his eye,
    Full sore itt him forethought.

The grayhound he wold not from his course fare;
Then was the King cast in care,
    And said, " Marroccke hath done me teene;
Slaine he hath a curteous knight,
And fained my Queene with great unright,
    As a traitor keene."

The King let draw anon-right
The stewards bodye, that false knight, 590
    With horsse through the towne;
Then he hanged him on a tree,
That all men might his body see,
    That he had done treason.
Sir Rogers body the next day
The King buryed in good array,
    With many a bold baron.

The grayhound was never away
By night nor yet by day,
    But on the ground he did dye. 600
The King did send his messengere
In everye place far and neere
    After the Queene to spye;
But for ought he cold enquire,
He cold of that Ladye nothing heare;
    Therfore the King was sorrye.

The King sayd, " I trow noe reed,
For well I wott that shee is dead;
    For sorrowe now shall I dye!
Alas, that ever shee from mee went!   610
This false steward hath me shent
    Throughe his false treacherye."

This King lived in great sorrow
Both evening and morrow
    Till that hee were brought to ground.
He lived thus many a yeere
With mourning and with evill cheere,
    His sorrowes lasted long:

And ever it did him great paine
When hee did thinke how Sir Roger was slaine,   620
    And how helped him his hound;
And of his Queene that was soe mylde,
How shee went from him great with child;
    For woe then did hee sound.

Long time thus lived the King
In great sorrow and mourning;
    And oftentime did weepe;
He tooke great thought more and more,
It made his hart verrye sore,
    His sighs were [f]ett soe deepe.   630

Now of the King wee will bline,
And of the Queene let us begin,
    And Sir Tryamore;
For when he was fourteen yeere old,
There was noe man soe bold
    Durst doe him dishonor;

In everye time both stout and stronge,
And in stature large and longe,
    Comlye of hye color;
All that ever he dwelled amonge,   640
He never did none of them wronge,
    The more that was his honor.

In that time sikerlye
Dyed the King of Hungarye
    That was of great age, I-wiss;
He had no heire his land to hold
But a daughter was fourteen yeers old;
    Faire *Hellen* shee named is.

Shee was as white as lilye flower,
And comely, of gay color,   650
    The fairest of any towne or tower;
Shee was well shapen of foote and hand,
Peere shee had none in noe land,
    Shee was soe fresh and soe amorous.

For when her father was dead,
Great warr began to spread
    In that land about;
Then the Ladyes councell gan her reade,
'Gett her a lord her land to lead,
    To rule the realme without doubt;   660
Some mightye prince that well might
Rule her land with reason and right,
    That all men to him might lout.'

And when her councell had sayd soe,
For great need shee had therto,
    Shee graunted them without lye:
The Lady said, "I will not feare
But he *be* prince or princes peere,
    And cheefe of all chivalrye."

Therto shee did consent,   670
And gave her lords commandement
    A great justing for to crye;
And at the justine, shold soe bee,
What man that shold win the degree,
    Shold win that Ladye trulye.

The day of justing then was sett,
Halfe a yeere without lett,
    Without any more delay,
Because they might have good space,
Lords, knights, dukes, in everye place,   680
    For to be there that day.

Lords, the best in everye land,
Hard tell of that rydand,
    And made them readye full gay;
Of everye land there was the best,
Of the States that were honest
    Attyred many a lady gay.

Great was that chivalrye
That came that time to Hungarye,
    There for to just with might.   690
At last Triamore hard tyding
That there shold be a justing;
    Thither wold he wend [right].

If he wist that he might gaine
With all his might, he wold be faine
    That gay Ladye for to win;
Hee had noe horsse nay noe other geere,
Nor noe weapon with him to beare;
    That brake his hart in twaine.

He thought both even and morrow 700
Where he might some armour borrowe,
    Therof wold hee be faine
To Sir Barnard then he can wend,
That he wold armour lend
    To just against the knights amaine.

Then said Sir Barnard, " What hast thou thought?
Pardew! of justing thou canst nought!
    For yee bee not able wepon to weld."
" Sir," said Triamore, " what wott yee
Of what strenght that I bee 710
    Till I have assayd in feeld? "

Then Sir Barnard that was full hend,
Said, " Triamor, if thow wilt wend,
    Thou shalt lacke noe weed;
I will lend thee all my geere,
Horsse and harneis, sheild and spere,
    Thou art nothing to dread;

" Alsoe thither with thee will I ryde,
And ever nye be by thy side
    To helpe thee if thou have need; 720
All things that thow wilt have,
Gold and silver, if thow wilt crave,
    Thy journey for to speed."

Then was Triamore glad and light,
And thanked Barnard with all his might
    Of his great proferinge.
That day the justing shold bee,
Triamore sett him on his knee
    And asked his mother blessinge.

At home shee wold have kept him faine;   730
But all her labor was in vaine,
    There might be noe letting.
Shee saw it wold noe better bee,
Her blessing shee gave him verelye
    With full sore weepinge.

And when it was on the morrow day,
Triamore was in good array,
    Armed and well dight;
When he was sett on his steed,
He was a man both lenght and bread,   740
    And goodlye in mans sight.

Then Triamore to the feeld can ryde,
And Sir Barnard by his side;
    They were jocund and light;
There was none in all the feild
That was more seemlye under sheild;
    He rode full like a knight.

Then was the faire Lady sett
Full hye uppon a turrett,
    For to behold that play;   750
There was many a seemlye knight,
Princes, lords, and dukes of might,
    Themselves for to assay,

With helme on theire heads bright
That all the feelds shone with light,
    They were soe stout and gay:
Then Sir Triamore and Sir Barnard
They pressed them into the feeld forward,
    There durst noe man say nay.

There was much price and pride 760
When everye man to other can ryde,
 And lords of great renowne;
It beffell Triamore that tyde
For to be on his fathers side,
 The King of Arragon.

The first that rode forth certainlye
Was a great lord of Lumbardye,
 A wonderfull bold barron.
Triamor rode him againe:
For all that lord had might and maine, 770
 The child bare him downe.

Then cryed Sir Barnard with honor,
" A Triamor, a Triamore!"
 For men shold him ken.
Mayd Hellen that was soe mild,
More shee beheld Triamore the child
 Then all the other men.

Then the Kings sonne of Navarrne
Wold not his body warne;
 He pricked forth on the plaine. 780
Then young Triamore that was stout,
Turned himselfe round about,
 And fast rode him againe;

Soe neither of them were to ground cast,
They sate soe wonderous fast,
 Like men of much might.
Then came forth a bachelour,
A prince proud without peere;
 Sir James, forsooth, he hight;

He was the Emperours sonne of Almaigne;   790
He rode Sir Triamore againe,
    With hard strenght to fight.
Sir James had such a stroake indeed
That he was tumbled from his steed;
    Then failed all his might.
There men might see swords brast,
Helmes ne sheilds might not last;
    And thus it dured till night;

But when the sun drew neere west,
And all the lords went to rest,   800
    Not so the maide Elyne.
The knights attired them in good arraye,
On steeds great, with trappers gaye,
    Before the sun can shine;

Then to the feeld they pricked prest,
And everye man thought himselfe best
    As the mayden faire they paste.
Then they feirclye ran together,
Great speres in peeces did shi[vv]er,
    Their timber might not last.   810

And at that time there did run
The King Arradas of Arragon :
    His sonne Triiamore mett him in that tyde,
And gave his father such a rebound
That harse and man fell to the ground,
    Soe stoutlye gan he ryde.

Then the next knight that hee mett
Was Sir James; and such a stroake him sett
    Upon the sheild ther on the plaine

That the blood brast out at his nose and eares,   820
His steed unto the ground him beares;
    Then was Sir Barnard faine.

That maid of great honor
Sett her love on younge Triamore
    That fought alwayes as a feirce lyon.
Speres that day many were spent,
And with swords there was many a stripe lent,
    Till there failed light of the sunne.

On the morrow all they were faine
    For to come into the feild againe   830
    With great spere and sheild.
Then the Duke of Siville, Sir Phylar,
That was a doughtye knight in everye warr,
    He rode first into the feild;

And Triamore tooke his spere,
Against the Duke he can it beare,
    And smote him in the sheild;
A-sunder in two peeces it went;
And then many a lovelye lady gent
    Full well they him beheld.   840

Then came forth a knight that hight Terrey,
Hee was a great lord of Surrey,
    He thought noble Triamore to assayle;
And Triamore rode to him bli[v]e
In all the strenght that he might drive,
    He thought he wold not fayle;

He smote him soe in that stond
That horsse and man fell to the ground,
    Soe sore his stroke he sett.

Then durst noe man att Triamore *ride*,   850
For fortune held all on his side
    All those dayes three.
Sir James, sonne unto the Emperour,
Had envye to Sir Triamore,
    And laid wait for him privilye.

Att the last Triamore came ryding bye:
Sir James said, " Triamore, thou shalt dye,
    For thou hast done me shame."
He rode to Triamore with a spere,
And thorrow the thigh he can him beare;   860
    He had almost him slaine.

But Tryamore hitt him in the head
That he fell downe starke dead.
    Then was all his men woe;
Then wold they have slaine Tryamore
Without he had had great succour;
    They purposed to doe soe.

With that came King Arradas then,
And reschued Tryamore with all his men,
    That stood in great doubt.   870
Then Sir Barnard was full woe
That Tryamore was hurt soe;
    Then to his owne house he him brought.

But when the mother saw her sonns wound,
Shee fell downe for sorrow to the ground,
    And after a leeche shee sent.
Of this, all the lords that were justinge,
To the pallace made highinge,
    And to that Ladye went.

Truly, as the Story sayes,   880
They pricked forth to the pallace
    The Ladyes will to heare,
Bachelours and knights prest,
That shee might choose of them the best
    Which to her faynest were.

The Ladye beheld all that fayre meanye,
But Tryamore shee cold not see :
    Tho chaunged all her cheere,
Then shee sayd, " Lord, where is hee
That everye day wan the degree ?   890
    I chuse him to my peere."

Al about they Tryamore sought ;
He was ryddn home ; they found him nought ;
    Then was that Ladye woe.
The knights were afore her brought,
And of respite shee them besought,
    A yeare and noe moe :

Shee said, " Lords, soe God me save !
He that wan me, he shall me have ;
    Ye wot well that my cry was soe."   900
They all consented her untill,
For shee said nothing ill,
    They said it shold be soe.

For when they had all sayd,
Then answered that fayre mayd,
    "I will have none but Tryamore."
Then all the lords that were present
Tooke their leave and home went ;
    There wan they litle honor.

Sir James men were nothing faine   910
Because their master he was slaine,
    That was soe stout in stowre;
In chaire his body they layd,
And led him home, as I have sayd,
    Unto his father the Emperour;

And when that hee his sonne gan see,
A sorrye man then was hee,
    And asked 'who had done that dishonor.'
They sayd, "Wee *ne* wott who it is, I-wisse,
But Sir Tryamore he named is,   920
    Soe they called him in the [stowre];

"The King of Arragon alsoe
He helped thy sonne to sloe,
    With all his companye."
They said, "They be good warryoirs;
They byte us with sharpe showers
    With great villanye."

"Alas!" said the Emperour,
"Till I be revenged on that traytour,
    Now shall I never cease!   930
They shall have many a sharpe shower,
Both the King and Tryamore,
    They shall never have peace!"

The Emperour sayd they shold repent;
And after great companye he sent
    Of princes bold in presse,
Dukes, earles, and lords of price.
With a great armye, the Duke sayes,
    They yeed to Arragon without lesse.

King Arradas was a-dread 940
For the Emperour such power had,
    That battell hee wold him bid;
He saw his land nye over-gon,
And to a castle hee fledd anon,
    And victualls it for dread.

The Emperour was bold and stout,
And beseeged the castle about;
    His banner he began to spread,
And arrayd his host full well and wiselye,
With wepons strong and mightye 950
    He thought to make them dread.

The Emperour was bold and stout,
And beseeged the castle about,
    And his banner he gan to spread;
He gave assault to the hold.
King Arradas was stout and bold,
    Ordayned him full well,

With gunes and great stones round
Were throwne downe to the ground,
    And on the men were cast; 960
They brake many backes and bones,
That they fought everye *day* ones
    While seven weekes did last.

The Emperour was hurt ill therfore,
His men were hurt sore,
    All his joy was past.
King Arradas thought full longe
That hee was beseeged soe stronge,
    With soe much might and maine:

Two lords forth a message he sent,   970
And straight to the Emperour they went,
    Soe when they cold him see,
Of peace they can him pray,
To take truce till a certaine day;
    They kneeled downe on their knee,

And said, "Our King sendeth word to thee
That he never your sonne did slay,
    Soe he wold quitt him faine;
He was not then present,
Nor did noe wise consent   980
    That your sonne was slaine.
That *he* will prove, if you will soe,
Your selfe and he betweene you tow,
    If you will it sayne;

"Or else take your selfe a knight,
And he will gett another to fight
    On a certaine day:
If that your knight hap soe
Ours for to discomfort or sloe,
    As by fortune itt may,   990
Our King then will doe your will,
Be att your bidding lowde and still
    Without more delay;

"And alsoe if it you betyde
That your knight on your syde
    Be slaine by mischance,
My lord shall make your warr to cease,
And we shall after be at pease,
    Without any distance."

The Emperour said without fayle
" Sett a day of battell
        By assent of the King of France ; "
For he had a great campiowne,
In everye realme he wan renowne ;
        Soe the Emperour ceased his distance.

When peace was made, and truce came,
Then King Arradas were a joyfull man,
        And trusted unto Tryamore.
Soe after him he went without fayle,
For to doe the great battelle
        To his helpe and succour.

His messengers were come and gone,
Tydings of him hard they none.
        The King Arradas thought him long,
" And he be dead, I may say ' alas ! '
Who shall then fight with Marradais
        That is soe stout and stronge ? "

When Tryamore was whole and sound,
And well healed of his wound,
        He busked him for to fare ;
He sayd, " Mother," with mild cheere,
" And I wist what my father were,
        The less were my care."

" Sonne," shee said, " thou shalt witt ;
When thou hast marryed that Ladye sweet,
        Thy father thou shalt ken."
" Mother," he said, " if you will *soe*,
Have good day, for now I goe
        To doe my masteryes if I can."

Then rode he over dale and downe   1030
Untill he came to Arragon,
        Over many a weary way.
Adventures many him befell,
And all he scaped full well,
        In all his great journey.

He saw many a wild beast
Both in heath and in forrest;
        He had good grey-hounds three;
Then to a hart he let them run
Till fourteen fosters spyed him soone,   1040
        Soe threatened him greatlye;

They yeede to him with weapons on everye side;
It was noe boote to bid them byde;
        Tryamore was loth to flye,
And said unto them, " Lords, I you pray,
Lett me in peace wend my way
        To seeke my grayhounds three."

Then said Tryamore as in this time,
" Gold and silver take all mine,
        If that I have trespassed ought."   1050

They said, " Wee will meete with th[ee] anon,
There shall noe gold borrow thee soone,
        But in prison thou shalt be brought,
Such is the law of the ground;
Whosoever therin may be found,
        Other way goe they nought."

Then Sir Tryamore was full woe
That to prison he shold goe;
   Hee thought the flesh to deare bought.
There was no more to say,   1060
The fosters att him gan lay
   With strokes sterne and stout.

There Tryamore with them fought;
Some to the ground be brought;
   He made them lowe to looke;
Some of them fast gan pray,
The other fled fast away
   With wounds wyde that they sought.

Tryamore sought and found his gray-hounds;
He hearkned to their yerning sounds,   1070
   And thought not for to leave them soe.
At last he came to a water side;
There he saw the beast abyde
   That had slaine two of his grayhounds;

The third full sore troubled the hind,
And he hurt him with his trinde;
   Then was Tryamore woe.
If the battaile had lasted a while,
The hart wold the hound beguile,
   And take his life for evermore.   1080

Tryamore smote att the deere,
And to the hart went the spere;
   Then his horne he blewe full sore.
The King lay there beside
At mannour that same tide;
   He hard a horne blowe;

They had great wonder in hall,
Both knights, squiers, and all,
    For noe man cold it know.
With that ran in a foster   1090
Into the hall with evill cheere,
    And was full sorry, I trow.

The King of tydings gan him fraine;
He answered, " Sir King, your keepers be slaine,
    And lye dead on a rowe.
There came a knight that was mightye,
He let three grayhounds that were wightye,
    And laid my fellowes full lowe."

He sayd it was full true
That the same that the horne blewe   1100
    That all this sorrow hath wrought.
King Arradas said then,
" I have great need of such of a man;
    God hath him hither brought."

The King commanded knights three;
He said, " Goe feitch yond gentleman to me
    That is now at his play;
Looke noe ill words with him yee breake,
But pray him with me for to speake;
    I trow he will not say nay."   1110

Everye knight his steed hent,
And lightlye to the wood they went
    To seeke Tryamore that child.
They found him by a water side
Where he brake the beast that tyde,
    That hart that was soe wylde.

They said, "Sir! God be at your game!"
He answered them even the same;
    Then was he frayd of guile.
"Sir knight!" they said, "is itt your will   1120
To come and speake our King untill
    With wordes meeke and mylde?"

Tryamore asked shortlye,
"What hight your King, tell yee mee,
    That is lord of this land?"
"This land hight Arragon,
And our King, Arradas, with crowne;
    His place is [n]eire att hand."

Tryamore went unto the King,
And he was glad of his cominge,   1130
    He knew him att first sight;
The King tooke him by the hand,
And said, "Welcome into this land!"
    And asked him what he hight.

"Sir, my name is Tryamore;
Once you helpt me in a stowre
    As a noble man of might;
And now I am here in thy land;
Soe was I never erst, as I understand,
    By God full of might."   1140

When the King wist it was hee,
His hart rejoiced greatlye;
    Three times he did downe fall,
And *said*, "Tryamore, welcome to me!
Great sorrowe and care I have had for thee;"
    And he told him all;

"With the Emperour I tooke a day
To defend me if that I may ;
⠀⠀⠀To Jesu I will call ;
For I never his sonne slew ;⠀⠀⠀⠀⠀⠀⠀⠀1150
God He knoweth I speake but true,
⠀⠀⠀And helpe me I trust He shall ! "

Then said Tryamore thoe, " *I am full woe*
That you for me have beene greeved soe,
⠀⠀⠀If I might it amend ;
And att the day of battell
I trust to prove my might as well,
⠀⠀⠀If God will grace me send."

Then was King Arradas very glad,
And of Marradas was not adread :⠀⠀⠀⠀⠀⠀1160
⠀⠀⠀When he to the batteile shold wend,
He joyed that he shold well speed,
For Tryamore was warry at neede
⠀⠀⠀Against his enemye to defend.

There Tryamore dwelled with the King
Many a weeke without lettinge ;
⠀⠀⠀He lacked right nought.
And when the day of battayle was c[o]me,
The Emperour with his men hasted full soone,
⠀⠀⠀And manye wonder thought ;⠀⠀⠀⠀⠀1170

He brought thither both King and knight ;
And Marradas, that was of might,
⠀⠀⠀To batteille he him brought.
There was many a seemelye man,
Moe then I tell you can ;
⠀⠀⠀Of them all he ne wrought.

176

Both partyes that ilke day
Into the feeld tooke the way,
　　They were already dight.
The King there kissed Tryamore,　　　　　　　　1180
And sayd, " I make thee mine *heyre* this hower,
　　And dubb thee a knight."

" Sir," said Tryamore, " take no dread;
I trust Jesus will me speede,
　　For you be in the right;
Therfore through Gods grace
I will fight for you in this place
　　With the helpe of our Lords might! "

Both partyes were full swore
To hold the promise that was made before;　　　1190
　　To Jesus can hee call.
Sir Tryamore and Sir Marradas
Both well armed was
　　Amonge the lords all;

Eche of them were sett on steede;
All men of Tryamore had dreede,
　　That was soe hind in all.
Marradas was stiffe and sure,
Their might noe man his stroake endure,
　　But that he made them fall.　　　　　　　　1200

Then rode they together full right;
With sharpe speres and swords bright
　　They smote together sore;
They spent speres and brake sheelds,
They busled fowle in middest the feelds,
　　Either fomed as doth a bore.

All they wondred that beheld
How they fought in the feeld;
   There was but a liffe.
Marradas fared fyer[y] wood   1210
Because Tryamore soe long stood;
   Sore gan hee smite.
Sir Tryamore fayled of Marradas,
That sword lighted upon his horsse,
   The sword to ground gan light.

Marradas said, " It is great shame
On a steed to wreake his g[r]ame!
   Thou sholdest rather smite mee! "
Tryamore swore, " By Gods might
I had lever it had on thee light!   1220
   Then I wold not be sorye;

" But here I give thee steede mine
Because I have slaine thine;
   By my will it shalbe soe."
Marradas sayd, " I will *him* nought
Till I have him with stroakes bought,"
   And won him from my foe.

And Tryamore lighted from his horsse,
And to Marradas straight he goes,
   For both on foote they did light.   1230
Sir Tryamore spared him nought,
But evyr in his hert he thoght
   " This day was I made a knight! "

And thought that hee himselfe wold be slaine soone,
" Or else of him I will win my shoone
   Throughe Gods might."
They laid eche at other with good will
With sharpe swords made of steele;
   That saw many a knight.

Great wonder it was to behold 1240
The stroakes that was betwixt them soe bold;
    All men might it see.
They were weary, and had soe greatlye bled;
Marradas was sore adread,
    He fainted then greatlye;

And that Tryamore lightlye beheld,
And fought feerclye in the feeld;
    He stroke Marradas soe sore
That the sword through the body ran.
Then was the Emperour a sorry man; 1250
    He made thenn peace for ever-more.

He kissed the King and was his freind,
And tooke his leavee homewards to wend;
    Noe longer there dwell wold hee.
Then King Arradas and Tryamore
Went to the palace with great honor,
    Into that rych citye.
There was joy without care,
And all they had great welfare,
    There might no better bee. 1260

They hunted and rode many a where,
Full great pleasure they had there.
    Among the knights of price
The King profered him full fayre,
And sayd, " Tryamore, Ile make thee mine heyre,
    For thou art strong and wise."

Sir Tryamore said, " Sir, trulye
Into other countryes goe will I;
    I desire of you but a steed,

And to other lands will I goe 1270
Some great adventures for to doe,
    Thus will I my liffe lead."
The King was verry sorry tho;
When that hee wold from him goe,
    He gave him a sure weede,

And plenty of silver and gold,
And a steed as hee wold,
    That nothing wold feare.
Hee tooke his leave of the King,
And mourned at his departing, 1280
    Then hasted he him there.

The King sayd, " Tryamor! that is mine,
When thou list it shall be thine,
    All my kingdome lesse and more."
Now is Tryamore forth goe;
Lords and ladyes were full woe,
    Everye man loved him there.

Tryamore rode in hast trulye
Into the land of Hungarye,
    Adventures for to seeke. 1290
Betweene two mountaines, the sooth to say,
He rode forth on his way;
    With a palmer he did meete;

He asked almes for Gods sake,
And Tryamore him not forgate,
    He gave him with words sweete.
The palmer said, " Turne yee againe,
Or else I feare you wilbe slaine;
    You may not passe but you be beat."

Tryamore asked, " Why soe ? "   1300
" Sir," he said, " there be brethren towe
        That on the mountaine dwells."
" Faith," said Tryamore, " if there be no more,
I trust in God that way to goe,
        If this be true that thou tells."
He bade the palmer good day,
And rode forth on his way
        Over heath and feelds ;

The palmer prayed to him full fast,
Tryamore was not agast,   1310
        He blew his horne full shrill.
He had not rydden but a while,
Not the mountenance of a mile,
        Two knights he saw on a hill :

The one of them to him gan ryde,
They other still gan abyde
        A litle there beside.
And when they did Tryamore spye,
They said, " Turne thee, traytor, or thou shalt dye,
        Therfore stand and abyde ! "   1320

Either againe other gan ryd fast,
Theire strokes mad their speres to brast,
        And made them wounds full wyde.
The other knight that hoved soe,
Wondred that Tryamore dared soe :
        He rode to them that tyde

And departed them in twaine,
And to speake fayre he began to fraine
        With words that sounded well :

To Tryamore he sayd anon,   1330
" A doughtyer knight I never saw none!
    Thy name that thou us tell."
Tryamore said, " First will I wett
Why that you doe keepe this street,
    And where that you doe dwell."

They said, " Wee had a brother hight Marradas,
With the Emperour forsooth he was,
    A stronge man well I-know.
In Arragon, before the Emperour,
A knight called Sir Tryamore   1340
    In battel there him slew;

" And alsoe wee say another,
Burlong our elder brother
    As a man of much might
He hath beseeged soothlye
The Kings daughter of Hungarye;
    To wed her he hath height;

" And soe well hee hath sped
That hee shall that Lady wedd
    But shee may find a knight   1350
That Burlonge overcome may;
To that they have tooke a day,
    Wage battel and fight;

" For that same Tryamore
Loved that Ladye paramoure,
    As it is before told;
If he will to Hungarye,
Needs must he come us by;
    To meete with him wee wold."

Tryamore said, " I say not nay,
But my name I will tell this day,
    In faith I will not laine :
Thinke your journey well besett,
For with Tryamore you have mett
    That your brother hath slaine."

" Welcome ! " they said, " Tryamore !
His death shalt thou repent sore ;
    Thy sorrow shall begin.
Yeeld thee to us anon,
For thou shalt not from us gone
    By noe manner of gin."

They smote feircly att him tho,
And Tryamore against them two
    Without more delay.
Sir Tryamore proved him full prest,
He brake their spere on their brest,
    Hee had such assay ;

His sheeld was broken in peeces three,
His horsse was smitten on his knee,
    Soe hard att him they thrust.
Sir Tryamore was then right wood,
And slew the one there as he stood
    With his sword full prest.

That other rode his way,
His hart was in great affray,
    Yet he turned againe that tide,—
When Tryamore had slaine his brother,
A sorry man then was the other,—
    And straight againe to him did rydde ;

Then they two sore foughte 1390
That the other to the ground was brought
    Then were they both slaine.

Tho the Ladye on Tryamore thought,
For of him shee knew right nought,
    Shee wist not what to say.
The day was come that was sett,
The lords assembled without lett,
    All in good array.

Burlonge was redye dight,
He bade the Lady send the knight. 1400
    Shee answered, " I ne may : "
For in that castle shee had hight
To keepe her with all her might.
    As the Story doth say.

They said, " If Tryamore be alive,
Hither will hee come bli[v]e;
    God send us good grace to speed ! "
With that came in Sir Tryamore
In the thickest of that stower,
    Into the feild without dread. 1410

He asked what all that did meane.
The people shewed that a battel there shold beene
    For the love of that Ladye.
He saw Burlong on his steede,
And straight to him he yeede;
    That Ladye challengeth hee.

Burlong asked him if he wold fight.
Tryamore said, " With all *my* might
    To slay thee, or thou me."
Anon they made them readye,   1420
And none there knew him sikerlye,
    They wondred what he shold bee.

High on a tower stood that good Ladye;
Shee knew not what knight verelye
    That with Burlong did fight.
Fast shee asked of her men
' If that knight they cold ken
    That to battell was dight;

' A griffon he beareth all of blew.'
A herald of armes soone him knew,   1430
    And said anon-right,
" Madame! God hath sent you succor;
For yonder is Tryamore
    That with Burlong will fight."

To Jesus gan the Ladye pray
For to speed him on his journey
    That hee about yeed.
Then those knights ran together,
The speres in peeces gan shiver,
    They fought full sore indeed;   1440

There was noe man in the feild tho
Whoe shold have the better of them tow,
    So mightilye they did them beare.
The battel lasted wonderous long;
Though Burlong was never soe stronge,
    There found he his peere.

2 B   185

Tryamore a stroke to him mint,
His sword fell downe at that dint
 Out of his hand him froe.
Then was Burlong verry glad,   1450
And the Ladye was verry sad,
 And many more full woe.

Tryamore asked his sword againe,
But Burlong gan him fraine
 To know first his name;
And said, " Tell me first what thou hight,
And why thou challengeth the Ladye bright,
 Then shalt thou have thy sword againe."

Tryamore sayd, " Soe mote I thee,
My name I will tell trulye,   1460
 Therof I will not doubt;
Men call me Sir Tryamore,
I wan this Ladye in a stowre
 Among barrons stout."

Then said Burlong, " Thou it was
That slew my brother Marradas!
 A faire hap thee befell ! "
Sir Tryamore sayd to him tho,
" Soe have I done thy brethren two
 That on the mountaines did dwell."   1470

Burlong said, " Woe may thou bee,
For thou hast slaine my brethren three !
 Sorrow hast thou sought !
Thy sword getts thou never againe
Till I be avenged, and thou slaine !
 Now I am well bethought ! "

Sir Tryamore sayd, " Noe force tho,
Thou shalt repent it ere thou goe ;
    Doe forth !   I dread thee nought ! "
Burlong to smite was readye bowne,   1480
His feete slipt, and hee fell downe,
    And Tryamore right well nought ;

His sword lightlye he up hent,
And to Burlonge fast he went ;
    For nothing wold he flee ;
And as he wold have risen againe,
He smote his leggs even in twaine
    Hard fast by the knee.

Tryamore bade him " Stand upright,
And all men may see now in fight   1490
    Wee beene meete of a size."
Sir Tryamore suffered him
To take another weapon,
    As a knight of much prize.

Burlong on his stumpes stood
As a man that was nye wood,
    And fought wonderous hard.
And Sir Tryamore strake stroakes sure,
For he cold well endure ;
    Of him hee was not affrayd,   1500

And under his ventale
His head he smote of without fayle ;
    With that in peeces his sword brast.

Now is Burlong slaine,
And Triamore with maine
　　Into the castle went,
To the Ladye that was full bright;
And att the gates shee mett the knight,
　　And in her armes shee him hent.

Shee said, " Welcome, Sir Tryamore!　　　1510
For you have bought my love full deere,
　　My hart is on you lent! "
Then said all the barrons bold,
" Of him wee will our lands hold; "
　　And therto they did assent.

There is noe more to say,
But they have taken a certaine day
　　That they both shalbe wed.
Sir Tryamore for his mother sent,
A messenger for her went,　　　　　　　1520
　　And into the castle her led.

Tryamore to his mother gan saine,
" My father I wold know faine,
　　Sith I have soe well sped."
Shee said, " King Arraydas of Arragon
Is thy father, and thou his owne sonne;
　　I was his wedded Queene;

" A leasing was borne me in hand,
And falsely fleamed me out of his land
　　By a traitor keene,　　　　　　　　1530
Sir Marrockee [he] hight : he did me woe,
And Sir Rodger my knight he did sloe,
　　That my guide shold have beene."

And when that Tryamore all heard,
And how his mother shee had sayd,
    Letters he made and wrought;
He prayd King Arradas to come him till,
If that it were his will,
    Thus he him besought:

'If hee will come into Hungarye   1540
For his manhood and his masterye,
    And that he wold fayle in nought.'
Then was King Arradas verry glad;
The messengers great guifts had,
    For they tydings that they brought.

The day was come that was sett,
The lords came thither without let;
    And ladyes of great pryde;
Then wold they noe longer lett;
Shortlye after they are fett,   1550
    With two dukes on everye side;

They lady to the church they led;
A bishopp them together did wed,
    In full great hast they hyed.
Soone after that weddinge
Sir Tryamore was crowned King,
    They wold noe longer abyde.

The Queene, his mother Margarett,
Before the King shee was sett
    In a goodlye cheare.   1560
King Arradas beheld his Queene,
Him thought that hee had her seene,
    Shee was a ladye fayre;
The King said, "It is your will
Your name me for to tell,
    I pray you with words fayre."

"My lord," sayd *she*, "I was your Queene;
Your steward did me ill teene;
    That evill might him befalle!"
The King spake noe more words   1570
Till the clothes were drawen from the bords,
    And men rose in the hall.
And by the hand he tooke the Queene gent;
Soe in the chamber forth he went,
    And there shee told him all.

Then was there great joy and blisse!
When they together gan kisse,
    Then all they companye made joy enough.
The younge Queene *was* full glad
That shee a kings sonne to her lord had,   1580
    Shee was glad, I trowe;

In joy together lead their liffe
All their dayes without striffe,
    And lived many a fayre yeere.
Then King Arradas and his Queene
Had joy enough them betweene,
    And merrilye lived together.

And thus wee leave of Tryamore
That lived long in great honor
    With the fayre Hellene.   1590
I pray God give their soules good rest,
And all that have heard this litle jest,
    Highe heaven for to win!
God grant us all to have that grace,
Him for to see in the celestyall place!
    I pray you all to say Amen!

ffinis

GUYE AND AMARANT

Guye journeyed ore the sanctifyed ground
 Wheras the Jewes fayre citye sometime stood,
Wherin our Saviours sacred head was crowned,
 And where for sinfull man He shed His blood.
To see the sepulcher was his intent,
The tombe that Joseph unto Jesus lent.

With tedious miles he tyred his wearye feet,
 And passed desarts places full of danger;
Att last with a most woefull wight did meet,
 A man that unto sorrow was noe stranger,   10
For he had fifteen sonnes made captives all
To slavish bondage, in extremest thrall.

A gyant called Amarant detained them,
 Whom noe man durst encounter for his strenght,
Who, in a castle which he held, had chaind them.
 Guy questions where, and understands at lenght
The place not farr. " Lend me thy sword," quoth Guy;
" Ile lend my manhood all thy sonnes to free."

With that he goes and layes upon the dore
 Like one, he sayes, that must and will come in.   20
The gyant, he was neere soe rowzed before,
 For noe such knocking at his gate had beene;
Soe takes his keyes and club, and goeth out,
Staring with irefull countenance about;

"Sirra!" sais hee, "what busines hast thou heere?
    Art come to feast my crowes about the walls?
Didst never heare noe ransome cold him cleere
    That in the compas of my furye falls?
For making me to take a porters paines,
With this same club I will dash out thy braines."   30

"Gyant," saies Guy, "your quarrelsome, I see;
    Choller and you are something neere of kin;
Dangerous at a club be-like you bee;
    I have beene better armed, though now goe thin.
But show thy utmost hate, enlarge thy spite!
Heere is the wepon that must doe me right."

Soe takes his sword, salutes *him* with the same
    About the head, the shoulders, and the sides,
Whilest his erected club doth death proclaime,
    Standing with huge collossous spacious strydes,   40
Putting such vigor to his knotted beame
That like a furnace he did smoke extreme.

But on the ground he spent his stroakes in vaine,
    For Guy was nimble to avoyde them still,
And ere he cold recovers clubb againe,
    Did beate his plated coate against his will:
Att such advantage Guy wold never fayle
To beate him soundly in his coate of mayle.

Att last, through strength, Amarant feeble grew,
    And said to Guy, "As thou art of humane race,   50
Shew itt in this, givee nature wants her dew;
    Let me but goe and drinke in younder place;
Thou canst not yeeld to *me* a smaller thing
Then to grant life thats given by the spring."

" I give the leave," sayes Guy, " goe drinke thy last,
    To pledge the dragon and the savage beare,
Suceed the tragedyes that they have past;
    But never thinke to drinke cold water more;
Drinke deepe to death, and after that carrouse
Bid him receive thee in his earthen house."   60

Soe to the spring he goes, and slakes his thirst,
    Takeing in the water in, extremly like
Some wracked shipp that on some rocke is burst,
    Whose forced bulke against the stones doe stryke;
Scoping it in soe fast with both his hands
That Guy, admiring, to behold him stands.

" Come on," quoth Guy, " lets to our worke againe;
    Thou stayest about thy liquor over longe;
The fish which in the river doe remaine
    Will want thereby; thy drinking doth them
              wrong;   70
But I will *have* their satisfaction made;
With gyants blood they must and shall be payd! "

" Villaine," quoth Amarant, " Ile crush thee straight!
    Thy life shall pay thy daring toungs offence!
This club, which is about some hundred waight,
    Has deathes commission to dispacth thee hence!
Dresse thee for ravens dyett, I must needs,
And breake thy bones as they were made of reeds! "

Incensed much att this bold Pagans bosts,
    Which worthy Guy cold ill endure to heare,   80
He hewes upon those bigg supporting postes
    Which like two pillars did his body beare.
Amarant for those wounds in choller growes,
And desperatelye att Guy his clubb he throwes,

2 c   193

Which did directlye on his body light
       Soe heavy and soe weaghtye there withall,
That downe to ground on sudden came the knight;
       And ere he cold recover from his fall,
The gyant gott his club againe in his fist,
And stroke a blow that wonderfullye mist.   90

"Traytor!" quoth Guy, "thy falshood Ile repay,
       This coward art to intercept my bloode."
Sayes Amarant, "Ile murther any way;
       With enemyes, all vantages are good;
O! cold I poyson in thy nostrills blowe,
Be sure of it, I wold destroy the soe!"

"Its well," said Guy, "thy honest thoughts appear
       Within that beastlye bulke where devills dwell,
Which are thy tennants while thou livest heere,
       But wilbe landlords when thou comest in hell.   100
Vile miscreant! prepare thee for their den!
Inhumane monster, hurtfull unto men!

"But breath thy selfe a time while I goe drinke,
       For flameing Pheabus with his fyerye eye
Torments me soe with burning heat, I thinke
       My thirst wold serve to drinke an ocean drye.
Forbear a litle, as I delt with thee."
Quoth Amarant, "Thou hast noe foole of mee!"

"Noe! sillye wretch! my father taught more
       How I shold use such enemyes as thou.   110
By all my gods! I doe rejoyce at itt,
       To understand that thirst constraines thee now?
For all the treasure that the world containes,
One drop of water shall not coole thy vaynes.

" Releeve my foe! why, twere a madmans part!
　　Refresh an adversarye, to my wronge!
If thou imagine this, a child thou art.
　　" No, fellow! I have knowne the world to longe
To be soe simple now I know thy want;
A minutes space to thee I will not grant."　　120

And with these words, heaving a-loft his club
　　Into the ayre, he swinges the same about,
Then shakes his lockes, and doth his temples rubb,
　　And like the Cyclops in his pride doth strout;
" Sirra," said hee, " I have you at a lifte;
Now you are come unto your latest shift;

" Perish for ever with this stroke I send thee,
　　A medcine will doe thy thirst much good;
Take noe more care of drinke before I end thee,
　　And then weelle have carowses of thy blood!　　130
Heeres at thee with a buchers downe-right blow,
To please my fury with thine overthrow!"

" Infernall, false, obdurat feend!" Guy said,
　　" That seemes a lumpe of crueltye from hell!
Ingratefull monster! since thou hast denyd
　　The thing to mee wherin I used thee *well*,
With more revenge then ere my sword did make,
On thy accursed head revenge Ile take!

" Thy gyants longitude shall shorter shrinke,
　　Except thy sunscorcht sckin doe weapon
　　　　prove.　　140
Farwell my thirst! I doe disdaine to drinke.
　　Streames, keepe your waters to your owne behoves,
Or let wild beasts be welcome therunto;
With those pearle dropps I will not have to doe.

" Hold, tyrant! take a taste of my good will;
　　For thus I doe begin my bloodye bout;
You cannot chuse but like the greeting ill;
　　It is not that same club will beare you out:
And take this payment on thy shaggye crowne,"—
A blow that brought him with a vengeance downe!　150

Then Guy sett foot upon the monsters brest,
　　And from his shoulders did his head devyde,
Which with a yawninge mouth did gape unblest,—
　　Noe dragons jawes were ever seene soe wyde
To open and to shut,—till liffe was spent.
Soe Guy tooke keyes, and to the castle went,

Where manye woefull captives he did find,
　　Which had beene tyred with extremitye,
Whom he in ffreindly manner did unbind,
　　And reasoned with them of their miserye.　160
Eche told a tale with teares and sighes and cryes,
All weeping to him with complainning eyes.

There tender laidyes in darke dungeon lay,
　　That were surprised in the desart wood,
And had noe other dyett everye day
　　Then flesh of humane creatures for their food;
Some with their lovers bodyes had beene fed,
And in their wombes their husbands buryed.

Now he bethinkes him of his being there,
　　To enlarge the wronged brethren from their
　　　　woes;　170
And as he searcheth, doth great clamors heare;
　　By which sad sounds direction, on he goes
Untill he findes a darkesome obscure gate,
Armed strongly over all with iron plate:

That he unlockes, and enters where appeares
    The strangest object that he ever saw,
Men that with famishment of many yeerres
    Were like deaths picture, which the painters draw;
Divers of them were hanged by eche thumbe;
Others, head downeward; by the middle, summe.   180

With dilligence he takes them from the walls,
    With lybertye their thraldome to accquainte.
Then the perplexed knight the father calls,
    And sayes, " Receive thy sonnes, thoe poore and
        faint!
I promised you their lives; eccept of that;
    But did not promise you they shold be fatt.

" The castle I doe give thee,—heere is the keyes,—
    Where tyranye for many yeeres did dwell;
Procure the gentle tender ladyes ease;
    For pittye sake use wronged women well!   190
Men may easilye revenge the deeds men doe,
But poore weake women have no strenght therto."

The good old man, even overjoyed with this,
    Fell on the ground, and wold have kist Guys feet.
" Father," quoth hee, " refraine soe base a kisse!
    For age to honor youth, I hold unmeete;
Ambitious pryd hath hurt me all it can,
I goe to mortifie a sinfull man."

ffinis

CALES VOYAGE

Att Cales wee latelye made afray,
Att Ile of Ree wee run away,
Our shippes poore Rochell did betray.
    Five subsiddyes for that,

And then wee shall to sea againe,
All that our generall was slaine,
And now wee have made peace with Spaine,
    Jacke ffellton!

Sir Artigall grand Torto slew;
Now everye man must have his dew   10
By vertue of a gracious new
    Petition of right.

The child of honor did deffye
In mortall fight his enemye,
And when he came to doe him dye,
    Cryes Sall Brooke.

Eleven children had Pope John,
Pope John the twelft, an able man;
Heeres to the daffe, Ile pledge the don,
    A pulpitt of sacke!   20

Noe more of that, doe not presume,
ffor ffeare of the Inquisition at Rome,
Where thou shalt find a cropeare dome,
    Cryes Layston.

Ten poundes for not being made a knight;
ffive thousand markes was deemed right
For being out of his countryes sight
    In time o shreavalltrye.

These and such like, as I you tell,
In Fayrye Land latelye befell,
Where Justice ffought with Justice Cell 30
    Att Gloster.

Be dutifull, good people all,
The government else alter shall,
And bring you to the state of Gaule,
    Haire shirts and woodden shooes!

Noe habeas corpus shall be gott;
But for all this damned plott
Tresilian went unto the pott
    Att Tyburne! 40

ffinis

KINGE AND MILLER

Henery, our royall King, wold goe a huntinge
    To the greene fforrest soe pleasant and fayre,
To have the harts chased, the daintye does tripping;
    To merry Sherwood his nobles repayre;
Hauke and hound was unbound, all things prepared
For the same to the game with good regard.

All a longe summers day rode the King pleasantlye
    With all his princes and nobles eche one,
Chasing the hart and hind and the bucke gallantlye,
    Till the darke evening inforced them turne
      home.   10
Then at last, ryding fast, he had lost quite
All his lords in the wood in the darke night.

Wandering thus wearilye all alone up and downe,
    With a rude miller he mett att the last,
Asking the ready way unto fayre Nottingham,
    " Sir," quoth the miller, " I meane not to jest,
Yett I thinke what I thinke truth for to say,
You doe not lightlye goe out of your way."

" Why, what dost thou thinke of me?" quoth our King
    merrily,
    " Passing thy judgment upon me soe breefe."   20
" Good faith," quoth the miller, "I meane not to flatter
    thee,
    I gesse thee to bee some gentleman theefe;
Stand thee backe in the darke! light not adowne,
Lest I presentlye cracke thy knaves crowne!"

"Thou doest abuse me much," quoth our King, "say-
  ing thus.
 I am a gentleman, and lodging doe lacke."
"Thou hast not," quoth the miller, "a groat in thy
  pursse;
 All thine inheritance hanges on thy backe."
"I have gold to discharge for that I call;
If itt be forty pence, I will pay all."   30

"If thou beest a true man," then said the miller,
 "I sweare by my tole dish Ile lodge thee all night."
"Heeres my hand," quoth our King, "that was I ever,"
 "Nay, soft," quoth the miller, "thou mayst be a
  sprite;
Better Ile know thee ere hands I will shake;
With none but honest men hands will I take."

Thus they went all alonge into the millers house,
 Where they were seeding of puddings and souce.
The miller first entered in, then after went the King;
 Never came he in soe smoakye a house. 40
"Now," quoth hee, "let me see heere what you are."
Quoth our King, "Looke your fill, and doe not spare."

"I like well thy countenance; thou hast an honest face;
 With my sonne Richard this night thou shalt lye."
Quoth his wiffe, "By my troth it is a good hansome
  youth;
 Yet it is best, husband, to deale warrilye.
Art thou not a runaway? I pray thee, youth, tell;
Show us thy pasport and all shalbe well."

Then our King presentlye, making lowe curtesie,
 With his hatt in his hand, this he did say: 50

" I have noe pasport, nor never was servitor,
　　But a poore courtyer rode out of the way ;
And for your kindnesse now offered to me,
I will requite it in every degree."

Then to the miller his wiffe whisperd secretlye,
　　Saing, " It seemeth the youth is of good kin
Both by his apparell and by his manners ;
　　To turne him out, certainely it were a great sin."
" Yea," quoth hee, " you may see hee hath some grace,
When as he speaks to his betters in place."　　60

" Well," quoth the millers wiffe, " younge man, welcome
　　　　heere !
And tho I sayt, well lodged shalt thou be ;
Fresh straw I will lay upon your bed soe brave,
　　Good browne hempen sheetes likwise," quoth shee.
" I," quoth the goodman, " and when that is done,
Thou shalt lye noe worse then our owne sonne."

" Nay first," quoth Richard, " good fellowe, tell me
　　　　true,
Hast thou noe creepers in thy gay hose ?
Art thou not troubled with the scabbado ? "
　　" Pray you," quoth the King, " what things are
　　　　those ? "　　70
" Art thou not lowsye nor scabbed ? " quoth hee ;
" If thou beest, surely thou lyest not with me."

This caused our King suddenly to laugh most heartilye
　　Till the teares trickled downe from his eyes.
Then to there supper were they sett orderlye,
　　To hott bag puddings and good apple pyes ;
Nappy ale, good and stale, in a browne bowle,
Which did about the bord merrilye troule.

" Heere," quoth the miller, " good fellowe, Ile drinke
  to thee
  And to all the courtnolls that curteous bee."   80
" I pledge thee," quoth our King, " and thanke thee
   heartilye
For my good welcome in everye degree ;
And heere in like manner I drinke to thy sonne."
" Doe then," saies Richard, " and quicke let it come."

" Wiffe," quoth the miller, " feitch me forth Lightfoote,
  That wee of his sweetnesse a litle may tast."
A faire venson pastye shee feiched forth presentlye.
  " Eate," quoth the miller, " but first make noe
   wast ;
Heer is dainty Lightfoote."   " Infaith," quoth our King,
" I never before eate of soe dayntye a thinge."   90

" Iwis," said Richard, " noe dayntye att all it is,
  For wee doe eate of it everye day."
" In what place," sayd our King, " may be bought lik
  to this ? "
  " Wee never pay peennye for it, by my fay ;
From merry Sherwood wee feitch it home heere ;
Now and then we make bold with our Kings deere."

" Then I thinke," quoth our King, " that it is venison."
  " Eche foole," " quoth Richard, " full well may
   see that ;
Never are we without two or three in the rooffe,
  Verry well fleshed and exellent ffatt.   100
But I pray thee say nothing where-ere thou goe,
We wold not for two pence the King shold it know."

" Doubt not," saies our King, " my promised secresye ;
  The King shall never know more ont for mee."

A cupp of lambes woole they dranke unto him,
 And to their bedds they past presentlye.
The nobles next morning went all up and downe
For to seeke the King in every towne;

At last, att the miller's house soone they did spye him
 plaine,
 As he was mounting upon his faire steede;   110
To whome they came presentlye, falling downe on their
 knees,
 Which made the millers hart wofullye bleed.
Shaking and quaking before him he stood,
Thinking he shold be hanged by the rood.

The King perceiving him fearfully tremblinge,
 Drew forth his sword, but nothing he said;
The miller downe did fall crying before them all,
 Doubtinge the King wold cut of his head.
But he, his kind curtesie for to requite,
Gave him great living, and dubd him a knight.   120

When as our noble King came from Nottingam,
 And with his nobles in Westminster lay,
Recounting the sports and the pastime they had tane
 In this late progresse along on the way;
Of them all, great and small, hee did protest
The miller of Mansfeild liked him best;

" And now, my lords," quoth the King, " I am deter-
 mined,
 Against St. Georges next sumptuous feast,
That this old miller, our youngest confirmed knight,
 With his sonne Richard, shalbe both my guest;   130
For in this merryment it is my desire
To talke with this jollye knight and the younge squier."

When as the noble lords saw the Kings merriment,
    They were right joyfull and glad in their harts.
A pursivant they sent straight on this busines,
    The which oftentimes used those parts;
When he came to the place where he did dwell,
His message merrilye then he did tell.

" God save your worshippe," then said the messenger,
    " And grant your Ladye her owne harts desire; 140
And to your sonne Richard good fortune and happinesse,
    That sweet younge gentleman and gallant squier!
Our King greets you well, and thus doth say,
' You must come to the court on St. Georges day ';

" Therfore in any case fayle not to be in place."
    " I-wis," quoth the miller, " it is an odd jest!
What shold wee doe there?" he sayd, "infaith I am
      halfe afraid."
    " I doubt," quoth Richard, " to be hanged att the
      least."
" Nay," quoth the messenger, " you doe mistake;
Our King prepares a great feast for your sake."   150

" Then," said the miller, " now by my troth, messenger,
    Thou hast contented my worshipp full well:
Hold! there is three farthings to quite thy great gentle-
      ness
    For these happy tydings which thou dost me tell.
Let me see! hearest thou me? tell to our King,
Weele wayte on his mastershipp in everye thing."

The pursivant smyled at their simplicitye;
    And making many leggs, tooke their reward,

And takeing then his leave with great humilitye,
    To the Kings court againe hee repayred,   160
Showing unto his Grace in everye degree
The knights most liberall giffts and great bountye.

When hee was gone away, thus can the miller say,
    " Heere comes expences and charges indeed!
Now must wee needs be brave, tho wee spend all wee
      have ;
    For of new garments wee have great need.
Of horsses and serving men wee must have store,
With bridles and sadles and twentye things more."

" Tushe, Sir John," quoth his wiffe, " neither doe frett
    nor frowne!
    You shall bee att noe more charges of mee!   170
For I will turne and trim up my old russett gowne,
    With everye thing else as fine as may bee ;
And on our mill horsses full swift wee will ryd,
With pillowes and pannells as wee shall provyde."

In this most statelye sort they rod unto the court,
    Their lusty sonne Richard formost of all,
Who sett up by good hap a cockes fether in his cappe ;
    And soe they jetted downe towards the Kings hall,
The merry old miller with his hands on his side,
His wiffe like Maid Marryan did mince at that tyde.   180

The King and his nobles that hard of their coming,
    Meeting this gallant knight with this brave traine,
"Welcome, sir knight," quoth hee, "with this your gay
      Lady!
    Good Sir John Cockle, once welcome againe ;
And soe is this squier of courage soe free ! "
Quoth Dicke, " A botts on you! doe you know me ? "

Quoth our King gentlye, " How shall I forgett thee ?
        Thou was my owne bed-fellow; well that I wot,
But I doe thinke on a tricke; tell me, pray thee, Dicke,
        How with farting we made the bed hott."   190
" Thou horson happy knave," then quoth the knight,
" Speake cleanly to our *King now*, or else goe shite ! "

The King and his councellors hartilye laugh at this,
        While the King tooke them by the hand.
With ladyes and their maids, like to the queene of spades
        The millers wiffe did most orderlye stand,
A milkemaids curtesye at everye word;
And downe these folkes were set to the bord,

Where the King royally with princely majestye
        Sate at his dinner with joy and delight.   200
When he had eaten well, to resting then hee fell;
        Taking a bowle of wine, dranke to the knight,
" Heeres to you both ! " he sayd, " in ale, wine, and beere,
Thanking you hartilye for all my good cheere."

Quoth Sir John Cockle, " Ile pledge you a pottle,
        Were it the best ale in Nottingam-shire."
" But then," said our King, " I thinke on a thinge,
        Some of your ' lightfoote ' I wold we had heere."
" Ho ! ho ! " quoth Richard, "full well I may say it;
Its knaverye to eate it and then to bewray it."   210

" What ! art thou hungry ? " quoth our King merrilye,
        " Infaith I take it verry unkind;
I thought thou woldest pledg me in wine or ale heartily."
        " Yee are like to stay," quoth Dicke, " till I have
                dind;
You feed us with twatling dishes soe small.
Zounds ! a blacke pudding is better then all."

" I, marry," quoth our King, " that were a daintye thing,
    If wee cold gett one heere for to eate."
With that, Dicke straight arose, and plucket one out of
    his hose,
    Which with heat of his breech began for to
        sweate.   220
The King made profer to snatch it away;
" Its meate for your master, good Sir; you shall stay!"

Thus with great merriment was the time wholy spent;
    And then the ladyes prepared to dance.
Old Sir John Cockle and Richard incontinent
    Unto this practise the King did advance,
Where-with the ladyes such sport they did make,
The nobles with laughing did make their heads ake.

Many thankes for their paines the King did give them
    then,
    Asking young Richard if he wold be wed :   230
" Amongst these ladyes faire, tell me which liketh
    thee."
    Quoth hee, "Jugg Grumball with the red head;
Shees my love; shees my liffe; her will I wed;
Shee hath sworne I shall have her maidenhead."

Then Sir John Cockle the King called unto him;
    And of merry Sherwood made him overseer,
And gave him out of hand three hundred pounds yearlye,
    " But now take heede you steale noe more of my
    deere!
And once a quarter lets heare have your vew;
And thus, Sir John Cockle, I bid thee adew!"   240

ffinis

AGINCOURTE BATTELL

A councell brave our King did hold
    With many a lord and knight,
In whom he trulye understands
    How ffrance withheld his right.

Therefor a brave embassador
    Unto the King he sent,
That he might ffully understand
    His mind and whole entente,

Desiring him, as freindlye sort,
    His lawfull wright to yeeld,   10
Or else he sware by dint of sword
    To win the same in feild.

The King of ffrance, with all his lords
    Who heard this message plaine,
Unto our brave embassador
    Did answer in disdaine;

Who sayd, " Our King was yett but younge
    And of a tender age;
Wherfor I way not for his warres,
    Nor care not for his rage,   20

" Whose knowledge eke in ffeats of armes,
    Whose sickill *is* but verry small,
Whose tender joynts more ffitter are
    To tosse a tennys ball."

A tunn of tennys balls therfore,
　　In pryde and great disdaine
He sends to noble Henery the Fifth,
　　Who recompenced his paine.

And when our King this message hard
　　He waxed wrath in his hart,
And said " he wold such balls provyde
　　That shold make all France to smart."

An army great our King prepared,
　　That was both good and strong;
And from Sowthampton is our King
　　With all his navye gone.

He landed in ffrance both safe and sound
　　With all his warlike traine;
Unto a towne called Harffleete first
　　He marched up amaine.

And when he had beseeged the same,
　　Against these fensed walls
To batter downe their statlye towers
　　He sent his English balls.

And he bad them yeeld *up to him*
　　Themselves and eke their towne,
Or else he sware unto the earth
　　With cannon to beate them downe.

The great gunn of Caleis was upsett,
　　He mounted against those walls;
The strongest steepele in the towne,
　　He threw downe bells and all.

30

40

50

Then those that were the governors
    Their woefull hands did wringe;
They brought their keyes in humble sort
    Unto our gracious King.

And when the towne was woone [at] last,
    The ffrenchmen out they threw,
And placed there three hundred Englishmen
    That wold to him be true.   60

This being done, our noble King
    Marched up and downe that land,——
And not a ffrenchman ffor his liffe
    Durst once his fforce withstand,——

Till he came to Agincourt;
    And as it was his chance,
To ffind the King in readinesse,
    With him was all the power of ffrance,

A mightye host they had prepared
    Off armed souldiers then,   70
Which was noe lesse (the Chronicle sayes)
    Then six hundred thousand men.

The King of ffrance, that well did know
    The number of our men,
In vaunting pride unto our King
    Sends one of his heralds then

To understand what he wold give
    For the ransome of his liffe,
When in that feild he had taken him
    Amiddst that bloody striffe.   80

And when our King the message heard,
    Did straight the answer make,
Saying, " Before that thing shold come to passe,
    Many of their harts shold ake!

" Unto your proud presumptuss Prince
    Declare this thing," quoth hee,
My owne harts blood shall pay the price;
    Nought else he getts of me."

Then all the night the Frenchman lyen,
    With triumphe, mirth, and joy;   90
The next morning they mad full accompt
    Our armye to destroye.

And for our King and all his lords
    At dice they playd apace,
And for our comon souldiers coates
    They set a prize but base,

Eight pence for a redd coate,
    And a groate was sett to a white;
Because they color was soe light,
    They sett noe better buy itt.   100

The cheerfull day at last was come;
    Our King with noble hart
Did pray his valliant soldiers all
    To play a worthye part,

And not to shrinke from fainting foes,
    Whose fearfull harts in ffeeld
Wold by their feirce couragious stroakes
    Be soone in-forced to yeeld;

" Regard not of their multitude,
    Tho they are more then wee,   110
For eche of us well able is
    To beate downe ffrenchmen three;

" Yett let everye man provide himselfe
    A strong substantiall stake,
And set it right before himselfe,
    The horsmans force to breake."

And then bespake the Duke of Yorke,
    " O noble King," said hee,
" The leading of that battell brave
    Vouchsafe to give it me ! "   120

" God amercy, cosen Yorke," sayes hee,
    " I doe grant thee thy request;
March you on couragiouslye,
    And I will guide the rest."

Then came the bragginge Frenchmen downe
    With cruell force and might,
With whome our noble King began
    A harde and cruell ffight.

Our English archers discharged their shafts
    As thicke as hayle in skye,   130
And many a Frenchman in that feelde
    That happy day did dye;

ffor the horssmen stumbled on our stakes,
    And soe their lives they lost:
And many a Frenchman there was tane
    For prisoners to their cost.

Ten thousand ffrenchmen there were slaine
    Of enemies in the ffeeld,
And neere as many prisoners tane
    That day were fforced to yeeld.   140

Thus had our King a happy day
    And victorye over ffrance ;
He brought his foes under his ffeete
    That late in pride did prance.

When they were at the maine battell there
    With all their might and forces, then
A crye came ffrom our English tents
    That we were robbed all them ;

For the Duke of Orleance, with a band of men,
    To our English tents they came ;   150
All our jewells and treasure that they have taken,
    And many of our boyes have slaine.

Much greeved was King Harry therat,—
    This was against the law of armes then,—
Comands everye souldier on paine of death
    To slay everye prisoner then.

Two hundred thousand ffrenchemen our Englishmen had,
    Some two, and some had one ;
Everye one was commanded by sound of trumpett
    To slay his prisoner then.   160

And then they followed upon the maine battell ;
    The ffrenchmen they fled then
Towards the citye of Paris
    As fast as they might gone.

But then ther was never a peere with-in France
    Of all those nobles then,
Of all those worthye Disse Peeres,
    Durst come to King Harry then.

But then Katherine, the Kings fayre daughter there,
    Being proved apparant his heyre,   170
With her maidens in most sweet attire
    To King Harry did repayre;

And when shee came before our King,
    Shee kneeled upon her knee,
Desiring him that his warres wold cease,
    And that he her love wold bee.

There-upon our English lords then agreed
    With the peeres of ffrance then;
Soe he marryed Katherine, the Kings faire daughter,
    And was crowned King in Paris then.   180

ffinis

CONSCIENCE

As I walked of late by one wood side,
    To God for to meditate was my entent,
Where under a hawthorne I suddenly espyed
    A silly poore creature ragged and rent;
    With bloody teares his face was besprent,
His fleshe and his color consumed away;
    With turning and winding his bodye was toste,
And his garments they were all mire, mucke, and clay.
" Good Lord! of my liffe deprive me, I pray,
    For I, silly wretch, am ashamed of my name!   10
My name," quoth hee, " is the cause of my care,
    And I cursse my godfathers that gave me the
        same!"

This made me muse, and much desire
    To know what kind of man hee shold bee;
I stept to him straight, and did him require
    His name and his secretts to shew unto me.
    His head he cast up, and wooful was hee,
" *My name,*" quoth hee, " *is the causer of my care,*
And makes me scornd, and left here soe bare."

Then straight-way he turnd him and prayd him sit
    downe,   20
" And I will," saithe he, " declare my whole greefe.
    My name is called ' Conscience ' "; wheratt he did
    frowne;
He pined to repeate it, and grinded his teethe.
        *   *   *
" For while I was young and tender of yeeres,
I was entertained with kings and with peeres,

" There was none in all the court that lived in such
         fame ;
     For with the Kings councell he sate in commission ;
Dukes, erles, and barrons esteemed of my name ;
     And how that I lived there needs no repetition ;
     I was ever holden in honest condition ;   30
For howsoever the lawes went in Westminster Hall,
When sentence was given, for me they wold call.

" Noe incombes at all the landlord wold take,
     But one pore peny, that was their fine,
And that they acknowledged to be for my sake ;
     The poore wold doe nothing without councell mine ;
     I ruld the world with the right line ;
For nothing that was passed betweene foe and freind,
But Conscience was called to bee at an end.

" Noe merchandize nor bargaines the merchants wold
         make,   40
     But I was called a wittenesse therto ;
No use for noe mony, nor forfett wold take,
     But I wold controwle them if that they did soe ;
     That makes me live now in great woe,
For then came in Pride, Sathans disciple,
That now is entertaind with all kind of people ;

He brought with him three, whose names they be these,
     That is Covetousnes, Lecherye, Usury, beside ;
They never prevailed till they had wrought my downe-
     fall ;
     Soe Pride was entertained, but Conscience was
        de[n]ide.   50
     Yet still abroad have I tryed
To have had entertainment with some one or other,
But I am rejected and scorned of my brother.

2 F   217

" Then went I to the court, the gallants to winn,
  But the porter kept me out of the gate.
To Bartl[m]ew Spittle, to pray for my sinne,
  They bad me ' goe packe ' me; it was fitt for my state;
    ' Goe, goe, threed-bare Conscience, and seeke thee
      a mate ! '
Good Lord, long preserve my King, Pirince, and
      Queene,
With whom ever more I have esteemed beene !   60

" Then went I to London, where once I did [dwell],
  But they bade away with me when they knew my
      name ;
' For he will undoe us to bye and to sell,'
  They bade me ' goe packe ' me, and hye me for shame,
  They lought at my raggs, and there had good game;
' This is old threed-bare Conscience that dwelt with St.
      Peeter ; '
But they wold not admitt me to be a chimney sweeper.

" Not one wold receive me, the Lord God doth know,
  I, having but one poore pennye in my pursse,
Of an aule and some patches I did it bestow ;   70
  I thought better to cobble shooes then to doe
      worsse.
  Straight then all the coblers they began to cursse,
And by statute they wold prove me I was a rouge and
      forlorne,
And they whipt me out of towne to see where I was
      borne.

" Then did I remember and call to my minde
  The Court of Conscience where once I did sit,
Not doubting but there some favor I shold find,
  For my name and the place agreed soe fitt.
  But therof my purpose I fayled a whitt,

For the judge did use my name in everye condicion, 80
For lawyers with their quilletts wold get a dismission.

" Then Westminster Hall was noe place for me ;
    Good God ! how the lawyers began to assemblee ;
And fearfull they were lest there I shold be !
    The silly poore clarkes began to tremblee ;
    I showed them my cause, and did not dissemble.
Soe then they gave me some mony my charges to beare,
But they swore me on a Booke I must never come
        there.

" Then the merchants said, ' Counterfeite, get thee
        away,
    Dost thou remember how wee thee found ?   90
We banisht thee the country beyond the salt sea,
    And sett thee on shore in the new-found land,
    And there thow and wee most freindly shook hands ;
And we were verry glad when thou did refuse us,
For when we wold reape proffitt heere thou wold
        accuse us.'

" Then had I noe way but for to goe an
    To gentlemens houses of ancyent name,
Declaring my greeffes ; and there I made moane,
    And how there forfathers had held me in fame,
    And in letting of their ffarmes I alwayes used
        the same.   100
They sayd, ' Fye upon thee ! we may thee cursse !
They have leases continue, and we fare the worsse.'

" And then I was forced a begging to goe
    To husbandmens houses ; who greeved right sore,
Who sware that their landlords had plaged them so,

That they were not able to keepe open doore,
　　Nor nothing they had left to give to the pore.
Therfore to this wood I doe repayre
With hepps and hawes; that is my best fare.

" And yet within this same desert some comfort I
　　　　have　　　　　　　　　　　　　　　110
Of mercy, of pittye, and of almes-deeds,
Who have vowed to company me to my grave.
　　Wee are ill put to silence, and live upon weeds;
　　　　*　　　　*　　　　*
Our banishment is their utter decay,
The which the rich glutton will answer one day."

"Why then," I said to him, " methinkes it were best
　　To goe to the Clergee; for dealye they preach
Eche man to love you above all the rest;
　　Of mercy and of pittie and of almes they doe teach."
　　" O," said he, " no matter of a pin what they
　　　　doe preach,　　　　　　　　　　　120
For their wives and their children soe hangs them
　　　　upon,
That whosoever gives almes deeds they will give none."

Then laid he him downe, and turned him away,
　　Prayd me to goe and leave him to rest,
I told him I might happen to see the day
　　To have him and his fellowes to live with the best;
" First," said hee, " you must banish Pride, and then
　　　　all England were blest,
And then those wold love us that now sells their lands,
And then good houses everye where wold be kept out of
　　　　hand."

ffinis

DURHAM FFEILDE

Lordinges, listen, and hold you still;
  Hearken to me a litle;
I shall you tell of the fairest battell
  That ever in England beffell.

For as it befell in Edward the Thirds dayes,
  In England, where he ware the crowne,
Then all the cheefe chivalry of England
  They busked and made them bowne;

They chosen all the best archers
  That in England might be found,   10
And all was to fight with the King of ffrance
  Within a litle stounde.

And when our King was over the water,
  And on the salt sea gone,
Then tydings into Scotland came
  That all England was gone;

Bowes and arrowes they were all forth,
  At home was not left a man
But shepards and millers both,
  And preists with shaven crownes.   20

Then the King of Scotts in a study stood,
  As he was a man of great might;
He sware 'he wold hold his Parlament in leeve London
  If he cold ryde there right.'

Then bespake a squier of Scottland borne,
    And sayd, " My leege, apace,
Before you come to leeve London
    Full sore youle rue that race!

" Ther beene bold yeomen in merry England,
    Husbandmen stiffe and strong;   30
Sharpes swords they done weare,
    Bearen bowes and arrowes longe.

The King was angrye at that word,
    A long sword out hee drew,
And there befor his royall companye
    His owne squier hee slew.

Hard hansell had the Scottes that day
    That wrought them woe enoughe,
For then durst not a Scott speake a word
    ffor hanging att a boughe.   40

" The Earle of Anguish, where art thou?
    In my coate armor thou shalt bee,
And thou shalt lead the forward
    Thorrow the English countrye.

" Take th[ee] Yorke," then sayd the King,
    " In stead wheras it doth stand;
Ile make thy eldest sonne after thee
    Heyre of all Northumberland.

" The Earle of Vaughan, where be yee?
    In my coate armor thou shalt bee;   50
The High Peak and Darbyshire
    I give it thee to thy fee."

Then came in [J]am[e]s Douglas,
 Saies, " What shall my meede bee
And Ile lead the vawward, Lord,
 Thorow the English countrye? "

" Take thee Worster," sayd the King,
 " Tuxburye, Killingworth, Burton upon Trent;
Doe thou not say another day
 But I have given thee lands and rent.   60

" Sir Richard of Edenborrow, where are yee,
 A wise man in this warr?
Ile give thee Bristow and the shire
 The time that wee come there.

" My Lord Nevill, where beene yee?
 You must in this warres bee!
Ile give thee Shrewsburye," saies the King,
 " And Coventrye faire and free.

" My Lord of Hambleton, where art thou?
 Thou art of my kin full nye;   70
Ile give thee Lincolne and Lincolneshire,
 And thats enouge for thee."

By then came in William Douglas
 As breeme as any bore;
He kneeled him downe upon his knees,
 In his hart he sighed sore,

Saies, " I have served you, my lovelye leege,
 This thirty winters and four,
And in the Marches betweene England and Scottland
 I have beene wounded and beaten sore; 80

" For all the good service that I have done,
    What shall my meed bee
And I will lead the vanward
    Thorrow the English countrye? "

" Aske on, Douglas," said the King,
    " And granted it shall bee."
" Why then, I aske litle London," saies William Douglas,
    " Gotten giff that it bee."

The King was wrath, and rose away,
    Saies, " Nay, that cannot bee!   90
For that I will keepe for my cheefe chamber,
    Gotten if it bee;

" But take thee North Wales and Weschaster,
    The cuntrye all round about,
And rewarded thou shalt bee,
    Of that take thou noe doubt."

Five score knights he made on a day,
    And dubbd them with his hands;
Rewarded them right worthilye
    With the townes in merry England.   100

And when the fresh knights they were made,
    To battell they buske them bowne;
James Douglas went before,
    And he thought to have wonnen him shoone.

But they were mett in a morning of May
    With the comminaltye of litle England;
But there scaped never a man away
    Through the might of Christes hand,

But all onely James Douglas;
    In Durham in the ffeild   110
An arrow stroke him in the thye.
    Fast flinges *he* towards the King.

The King looked toward litle Durham,
    Saies, " All things is not well!
For James Dowglas beares an arrow in his thye,
    The head of it is of steele.

" How now, James ? " then said the King,
    " How now, how may this bee ?
And where beene all thy merrymen
    That thou tooke hence with thee ? "   120

" But cease, my King," saies James Douglas,
    " Alive is not left a man! "
" Now by my faith," saies the King of Scottes,
    " That gate was evill gone;

" But Ile revenge thy quarrell well,
    And of that thou may be faine;
For one Scott will beate five Englishmen
    If they meeten them on the plaine."

" Now hold your tounge," saies James Douglas,
    " For in faith that is not soe;   130
For one English man is worth five Scotts
    When they meeten together thoe;

" For they are as egar men to fight
    As a faulcon upon a pray.
Alas! if ever they winne the vanward,
    There scapes noe man away."

"O peace thy talking," said the King,
  "They bee but English knaves,
But shepards and millers both,
  And *mass* preists with their staves."   140

The King sent forth one of his heralds of armes
  To vew the Englishmen.
"Be of good cheere," the herald said,
  "For against one wee bee ten."

"Who leades those ladds?" said the King of Scottes,
  "Thou herald, tell thou mee."
The herald said, "The Bishopp of Durham
  Is captaine of that companye;

"For the Bishopp hath spred the Kings banner
  And to battell he buskes him bowne."   150
"I sweare by St. Andrewes bones," saies the King,
  "Ile rapp that preist on the crowne!"

Second Part

The King looked towards litle Durham,
  And that hee well beheld,
That the Earle Percy was well armed,
  With his battell axe entred the feild.

The King looket againe towards litle Durham,
  Four ancyents there see hee;
There were to standards, six in a valley,
  He cold not see them with his eye.   160

My Lord of Yorke was one of them,
　　My Lord of Carlile was the other;
And my Lord ffluwilliams,
　　The one came with the other.

The Bishopp of Durham commanded his men,
　　And shortlye he them bade,
'That never a man shold goe to the feild to fight
　　Till he had served his God.'

Five hundred preists said masse that day
　　In Durham in the feild;　　　　　　170
And afterwards, as I hard say,
　　They bare both speare and sheeld.

The Bishopp of Durham orders himselfe to fight
　　With his battell axe in his hand;
He said, " This day now I will fight
　　As long as I can stand!"

" And soe will I," sayd my Lord of Carlile,
　　In this faire morning gay;"
" And soe will I," said my Lord ffluwilliams,
　　" For Mary, that myld may."　　　　180

Our English archers bent their bowes
　　Shortlye and anon,
They shott over the Scottish oast
　　And scantlye toucht a man.

" Hold downe your hands," sayd the Bishopp of Durham,
　　" My archers good and true."
The second shoote that they shott,
　　Full sore the Scottes itt rue.

The Bishopp of Durham spoke on hye,
 That both partyes might heare,   190
" Be of good cheere, my merrymen all,
 The Scotts flyen, and changen there cheere!"

But as they saidden, soe they didden,
 They fell on heapes hye;
Our Englishmen laid on with their bowes
 As fast as they might dree.

The King of Scotts in a studye stood
 Amongst his companye,
An arrow stoke him thorrow the nose
 And thorrow his armorye.   200

The King went to a marsh side
 And light beside his steede,
He leaned him downe on his sword hilts
 To let his nose bleede.

There followed him a yeaman of merry England,
 His name was John of Coplande:
" Yeeld thee, traytor!" saies Coplande then,
 " Thy liffe lyes in my hand."

" How shold I yeeld me," says the King,
 " And thou art noe gentleman?"   210
" Noe, by my troth," sayes Copland there,
 " I am but a poore yeaman;

" What art thou better then I, Sir King?
 Tell me if that thou can!
What art thou better then I, Sir King,
 Now we be but man to man?"

The King smote angerly at Copland then,
    Angerly in that stonde;
And then Copland was a bold yeaman,
    And bore the King to the ground.   220

He sett the King upon a palfrey,
    Himselfe upon a steede,
He tooke him by the bridle rayne,
    Towards London he can him lead.

And when to London that he came,
    The King from ffrance was new come home,
And there unto the King of Scottes
    He sayd these words anon,

" How like you my shepards and my millers,
    My priests with shaven crownes? "   230
" By my fayth, they are the sorest fighting men
    That ever I mett on the ground;

" There was never a yeaman in merry England,
    But he was worth a Scottish knight! "
" I, by my troth," said King Edward, and laughe,
    " For you fought all against the right."

But now the Prince of merry England
    Worthilye under his sheelde
Hath taken the King of ffrance
    At Poytiers in the ffeelde. ·   240

The Prince did present his father with that food,
    The lovely King off ffrance,
And fforward of his journey he is gone:
    God send us all good chance!

"You are welcome, brother!" sayd the King of Scotts,
    "For I am come hither to soone;
Christ leeve that I had taken my way
    Unto the court of Roome!"

"And soe wold I," said the King of ffrance,
    "When I came over the streame,   250
That I had taken my journey
    Unto Jerusalem."

Thus ends the battell of ffaire Durham
    In one morning of May,
The battell of Cressey, and the battle of Potyers,
    All within one monthes day.

Then was welthe and welfare in mery England,
    Solaces, game, and glee,
And every man loved other well,
    And the King loved good yeomanrye.   260

But God, that made the grasse to growe,
    And leaves on greenwoode tree,
Now save and keepe our noble King,
    And maintaine good yeomanry!

ffinis

GUY AND PHILLIS

In Winsor fforrest I did slay
    A bore of passing might and strenght,
Whose like in England never was
    For hugnesse, both for breadth and lenght;

Some of his bones in Warwicke yett
    Within the Castle there doth lye;
One of his sheeld bones to this day
    Doth hang in the citye of Coventrye.

On Dunsmore Heath I alsoe slewe
    A mightye wyld and cruell beast   10
Calld the Duncow of Dunsmore Heath,
    Which many people had opprest;

Some of her bones in Warwicke yett
    There for a monument doth lye,
Which unto every lookers veue
    As wonderous strange they may espye.

Another dragon in this land
    In fight I alsoe did destroye,
Who did bothe men and beasts opresse,
    And all the countrye sore anoye;   20

And then to Warwicke came againe
    Like pilgrim poore, and was not knowen;
And there I lived a hermitts liffe,
    A mile and more out of the towne;

Where with my hands I hewed a house
    Out of a craggy rocke of stone,
And lived like a palmer poore
    Within the cave my selfe alone;

And daylye came to begg my foode
    Of Phillis att my castle gate,   30
Not knowing to my loved wiffe,
    Who daylye moned for her mate;

Till att the last I fell soe sicke,
    Yea, sicke soe sore that I must dye.
I sent to her a ring of gold
    By which shee knew me presentlye;

Then shee, repairing to the [c]ave,
    Befor that I gave up the ghost
Shee closed up my dying eyes,
    My Phillis faire, whom I loved most.   40

Thus dreadfull death did me arrest,
    To bring my corpes unto the grave;
And like a palmer dyed I,
    Wherby I sought my soule to save.

My body that endured this toyle,
    Tho now it be consumed to mold,—
My statue ingraven in [stone]
    This present time you may behold.

ffinis

JOHN : A : SIDE

Peeter a Whifeild he hath slaine;
 And John a Side, he is tane;
And John is bound both hand and foote,
 And to the New-castle he is g[a]ne.

But tydinges came to the Sybill o the Side,
 By the water side as shee rann;
Shee tooke her kirtle by the hem,
 And fast shee runn to Mangerton.

    *   *   *

 The lord was sett downe at his meate;
When these tydings shee did him tell,   10
 Never a morsell might he eate.

But lords they wrunge their fingars white,
 Ladyes did pull themselves by the haire,
Crying, "Alas, and weladay!
 For John o the Side wee shall never see more!

" But weele goe sell our droves of kine,
 And after them our oxen sell,
And after them our troopes of sheepe,
 But wee will loose him out of the New-castell."

But then bespake him Hobby Noble,   20
 And spoke these words wonderous hye,
Sayes," Give me five men to my selfe,
 And Ile feitch John o the Side to thee."

"Yea, thoust have five, Hobby Noble,
    Of the best that are in this countrye!
Ile give thee five thousand, Hobby Noble,
    That walke in Tyvidale trulye."

" Nay, Ile have but five," saies Hobby Noble,
    " That shall walke away with mee;
Wee will ryde like noe men of warr;   30
    But like poore badgers wee wilbe."

They stuffet up all their baggs with straw,
    And their steeds barefoot must bee;
" Come on, my bretheren," sayes Hobby Noble,
    " Come on your wayes, and goe with mee."

And when they came to Culerton Ford,
    The water was up, they cold it not goe;
And then they were ware of a good old man,
    How his boy and hee were at the plowe.

" But stand you still," sayes Hobby Noble,   40
    " Stand you still heere at this shore,
And I will ryde to yonder old man,
    And see were the gate it lyes ore.

" But Christ you save, father," quoth hee,
    Crist both you save and see!
Where is the way over this fford?
    For Christs sake tell itt mee!"

" But I have dwelled heere three score yeere,
    Soe have I done three score and three;
I never sawe man nor horsse goe ore   50
    Except itt were a horse of three."

"But fare thou well, thou good old man;
      The devill in hell I leave with thee!
Noe better comfort heere this night
      Thow gives my bretheren heere and me."

But when he came to his brether againe,
      And told this tydings full of woe,
And then they found a well good gate
      They might ryde ore by two and two.

And when they were come over the fforde,   60
      All safe gotten att the last,
"Thankes be to God!" sayes Hobby Nobble,
      The worst of our perill is past."

And then they came into Howbrame Wood,
      And there then they found a tree,
And cutt itt downe then by the roote;
      The lenght was thirty ffoote and three.

And four of them did take the planke
      As light as it had beene a fflee,
And carryed itt to the Newcastle   70
      Where as John a Side did lye:

And some did climbe up by the walls,
      And some did climbe up by the tree,
Untill they came upp to the top of the Castle
      Where John made his moane trulye:

He sayd, "God be with thee, Sybill o the Side!
      My owne mother thou art," quoth hee,
"If thou knew this knight I were here,
      A woe woman then woldest thou bee!

"And fare you well, Lord Mangerton!   80
    And ever I say 'God be with thee!'
For if you knew this night I were heere,
    You wold sell your land for to loose mee.

"And fare thou well, Much Millers sonne!
    Much Millars sonne, I say;
Thou has beene better at merke midnight
    Then ever thou was att noone o the day.

"And fare thou well, my good Lord Clough!
    Thou art thy ffathers sonne and heire;
Thou never saw him in all thy liffe,   90
    But with him durst thou breake a speare.

"Wee are brothers childer nine or ten,
    And sisters children ten or eleven;
We never come to the feild to fight,
    But the worst of us was counted a man."

But then bespake him Hoby Noble,
    And spake these words unto him,
"Saies, "Sleepest thou, wakest thou, John o the Side,
    Or art thou this Castle within?"

"But who is there," quoth John oth Side,   100
    "That knowes my name soe right and free?"
"I am a bastard brother of thine;
    This night I am comen for to loose thee."

"Now nay, now nay," quoth John othe Side,
    "Itt ffeares me sore that will not bee;
ffor a pecke of gold and silver," John sayd,
    "Infaith this night will not loose mee."

But then bespake him Hobby Noble,
    And till his brother thus sayd hee,
Sayes, " Four shall take this matter in hand,   110
    And two shall tent our geldings ffree."

For four did breake one dore without,
    Then John brake five himsell;
But when they came to the iron dore,
    It smote twelve upon the bell.

" Itt ffeares me sore," sayd Much the Miller,
    " That heere taken wee all shalbee."
" But goe away, bretheren," sayd John a Side,
    " For ever, alas! this will not bee."

" But ffye upon thee!" sayd Hobby Noble;   120
    " Much the Miller! fye upon thee!
" It sore feares me," said Hobby Noble,
    " Man that thou wilt never bee."

But then he had fflanders files two or three,
    And hee fyled downe that iron dore,
And tooke John out of the New-castle,
    And sayd, " Looke thou never come heere more!"

When he had him fforth of the Newcastle,
    " Away with me, John, thou shalt ryde."
But ever alas! itt cold not bee;   130
    For John cold neither sitt nor stryde.

But then he had sheets two or three,
    And bound Johns boults fast to his ffeete,
And sett him on a well good steede,
    Himselfe on another by him seete.

Then Hobby Noble smiled and louge,
 And spoke these words in mickle pryde,
" Thou sitts soe finely on thy geldinge
 That, John, thou rydes like a bryde."

And when they came thorrow Howbrame towne,   140
 Johns horsse there stumbled at a stone;
" Out and alas!" cryed Much the Miller,
 " John, thoule make us all be tane."

" But fye upon thee!" saies Hobby Noble,
 " Much the Millar, fye on thee!
I know full well," says Hobby Noble,
 " Man that thou wilt never bee!"

And when they came into Howbrame wood,
 He had fflanders files two or three
To file Johns bolts beside his ffeete,   150
 That hee might ryde more easilye.

Sayes John, " Now leape over a steede,"
 And John then hee lope over five:
" I know well," sayes Hobby Noble,
 " John, thy fellow is not alive!"

Then he brought him home to Mangerton;
 The lord then he was att his meate;
But when John o the Side he there did see,
 For faine hee cold noe more eate;

He sayes, " Blest be thou, Hobby Noble,   160
 That ever thou wast man borne!
Thou hast feitched us home good John oth Side
 That was now cleane ffrom us gone!"

ffinis

RISINGE IN THE NORTHE

Listen, lively lordings all,
    And all that beene this place within!
If youle give eare unto my songe,
    I will tell you how this geere did begin.

It was the good Erle of Westmorlande,
    A noble erle was called hee;
And he wrought treason against the crowne;
    Alas, itt was the more pittye!

And soe itt was the Erle of Northumberland,   10
    Another good noble erle was hee,
They tooken both upon one part,
    Against their crowne they wolden bee.

Earle Pearcy is into his garden gone,
    And after walkes his awne ladye;
" I heare a bird sing in my eare
    That I must either ffight or fflee."

" God fforbidd," shee sayd, " good my lord,
    That ever soe that it shalbee!
But goe to London to the court,
    And faire ffall truth and honestye!"   20

" But nay, now nay, my ladye gay,
    That ever it shold soe bee;
My treason is knowen well enoughe;
    Att the court I must not bee."

" But goe to the court yet, good my lord,
    Take men enowe with thee ;
If any man will doe you wronge,
    Your warrant they may bee."

" But nay, now nay, my lady gay,
    For soe itt must not bee ;   30
If I goe to the court, ladye,
    Death will strike me, and I must dye."

" But goe to the court yett, *good* my lord,
    I my-selfe will ryde with thee ;
If any man will doe you wronge,
    Your borrow I shalbee."

" But nay, now nay, my lady gay,
    For soe it must not bee ;
For if I goe to the court, ladye,
    Thou must me never see.   40

" But come hither, thou litle footpage,
    Come thou hither unto mee,
For thou shalt goe a message to Master Norton
    In all the hast that ever may bee :

" Comend me to that gentleman ;
    Bring him here this letter from mee,
And say, ' I pray him earnestlye
    That hee will ryde in my companye.' "

But one while the foote page went,
    Another while he rann ;   50
Untill he came to Master Norton,
    The ffoot page never blanne ;

And when he came to Master Nortton,
 He kneeled on his knee,
And tooke the letter betwixt his hands,
 And lett the gentleman it see.

And when the letter itt was reade
 Affore all his companye,
I-wis, if you wold know the truth,
 There was many a weeping eye.   60

He said, " Come hither, Kester Nortton,
 A ffine ffellow thou seemes to bee ;
Some good councell, Kester Nortton,
 This day doe thou give to mee."

" Marry, Ile give you councell, ffather,
 If youle take councell att me,
That if you have spoken the word, father,
 That backe againe you doe not flee."

" God amercy, Christopher Nortton,
 I say, God amercye !   70
If I doe live and scape with liffe,
 Well advanced shalt thou bee ;

" But come you hither, my nine good sonnes,
 In mens estate I thinke you bee ;
How many of you, my children deare,
 On my part that wilbe ? "

But eight of them did answer soone,
 And spake ffull hastilye,
Sayes, " We wilbe on your part, ffather,
 Till the day that we doe dye."   80

" But God amercy, my children deare,
    And ever I say Godamercy!
And yett my blessing you shall have,
    Whether-soever I live or dye.

" But what sayst thou, thou ffrancis Nortton,
    Mine eldest sonne and mine heyre trulye?
Some good councell, ffrancis Nortton,
    This day thou give to me."

" But I will give you councell, ffather,
    If you will take councell att mee;   90
For if you wold take my councell, father,
    Against the crowne you shold not bee."

" But ffye upon thee, ffrancis Nortton!
    I say ffye upon thee!
When thou was younge and tender of age
    I made ffull much of thee."

" But your head is white, ffather," he sayes,
    "And your beard is wonderous gray;
Itt were shame ffor your countrye
    If you shold rise and fflee away."   100

" But ffye upon thee, thou coward ffrancis!
    Thou never tookest that of mee!
When thou was younge and tender of age
    I made too much of thee."

" But I will goe with you, father," quoth hee;
    "Like a naked man will I bee;
He that strikes the first stroake against the crowne,
    An ill death may hee dye!"

But then rose upp Master Nortton that esquier,
　　With him a ffull great companye;　　　　　110
And then the erles they comen downe
　　To ryde in his companye.

Att Whethersbye they mustered their men
　　Upon a ffull fayre day;
Thirteen thousand there were seene
　　To stand in battel ray.

The Erle of Westmoreland, he had in his ancyent
　　The Dume Bull in sight most hye,
And Three Doggs with golden collers
　　Were sett out royallye.　　　　　120

The Erle of Northumberland, he had in his ancyent
　　The Halfe Moone in sight soe hye,
As the Lord was crucifyed on the crosse,
　　And sett forthe pleasantlye.

And after them did rise good Sir George Bowes,
　　After them a spoyle to make;
The erles returned backe againe,
　　Thought ever that knight to take.

This barron did take a castle then,
　　Was made of lime and stone;　　　　　130
The uttermost walls were ese to be woon;
　　The erles have woon them anon;

But tho they woone the uttermost walls
　　Quickly and anon,
The innermust walles they cold not winn,
　　They were made of a rocke of stone.

243

But newes itt came to leeve London
    In all they speede that ever might bee;
And word it came to our royall Queene
    Of all the rebells in the north countrye.   140

Shee turned Her Grace then once about,
    And like a royall Queene shee sware,
Sayes, " I will ordaine them such a breake-fast
    As was not in the north this thousand yeere!"

Shee caused thirty thousand men to be made
    With horsse and harneis all quicklye;
And shee caused thirty thousand men to be made
    To take the rebells in the north countrye.

They tooke with them the false Erle of Warwicke,
    Soe did they many another man;   150
Untill they came to Yorke castle,
    I-wis, they never stinted nor blan.

" Spread thy ancyent, Erle of Westmoreland!
    The Halfe Moone ffaine wold wee see!"
But the Halfe Moone is fled and gone,
    And the Dun Bull vanished awaye;
And ffrancis Nortton and his eight sonnes
    Are ffled away most cowardlye.

Ladds with mony are counted men,
    Men without mony are counted none;   160
But hold your tounge! why say you soe?
    Men wilbe men when mony is gone.

ffinis

244

NORTHUMBERLAND BETRAYD BY DOWGLAS

Now list and lithe you, gentlemen,
　　And Ist tell you the veretye,
How they have delt with a banished man,
　　Driven out of his countrye.

When as hee came on Scottish ground,
　　As woe and wonder be them amonge,
ffull much was there traitorye
　　They wrought the Erle of Northumberland.

When they were att the supper sett,
　　Beffore many goodly gentlemen　　　　　　10
They ffell a fflouting and mocking both,
　　And said to the Erle of Northumberland,

"What makes you be soe sad, my Lord,
　　And in your mind soe sorrowffullye?
In the north of Scottland to-morrow theres a shooting,
　　And thither thoust goe, my Lord Percye.

"The buttes are sett, and the shooting is made,
　　And there is like to be great royaltye,
And I am sworne into my bill
　　Thither to bring my Lord Pearcy."　　　　　20

"Ile give thee my land, Douglas," he sayes,
　　And be the faith in my bodye,
If that thou wilt ryde to the worlds end,
　　Ile ryde in thy companye."

And then bespake the good Ladye,—
　　Marry a Douglas was her name,—
"You shall byde here, good English lord;
　　My brother is a traiterous man;

"He is a traitor stout and stronge,
    As Ist tell you the veretye,   30
For he hath tane liverance of the Erle,
    And into England he will livor thee."

"Now hold thy tounge, thou goodlye Ladye,
    And let all this talking bee;
ffor all the gold thats in Loug Leven,
    William wold not livor mee!

"It wold breake truce betweene England and Scottland,
    And freinds againe they wold never bee
If he shold livor a banisht Erle
    Was driven out of his owne countrye."   40

"Hold your tounge, my Lord," shee sayes,
    "There is much ffalsehood them amonge;
When you are dead, then they are done,
    Soone they will part them freinds againe.

"If you will give me any trust, my Lord,
    Ile tell you how you best may bee;
Youst lett my brother ryde his wayes,
    And tell those English lords trulye

How that you cannot with them ryde
    Because you are in an ile of the sea;   50
Then, ere my brother come againe,
    To Edenborrow Castle Ile carry thee;

"Ile livor you unto the Lord Hume,
    And you know a trew Scothe lord is hee,
For he hath lost both land and goods
    In ayding of your good bodye."

"Marry, I am woe! woman," he sayes,
    "That any freind fares worse for mee;
For where one saith 'It is a true tale,'
    Then two will say 'It is a lye.'   60

"When I was att home in my *realme*,
    Amonge my tennants all trulye,
In my time of losse, wherin my need stoode,
    They came to ayd me honestlye;

"Therfore I left many a child ffatherlese,
    And many a widdow to looke wanne;
And therfore blame nothing, Ladye,
    But the woeffull warres which I began."

"If you will give me noe trust, my Lord,
    Nor noe credence you will give mee,   70
And youle come hither to my right hand,
    Indeed, my Lord, Ile lett you see."

Saies, "I never loved noe witchcraft,
    Nor never dealt with treacherye,
But evermore held the hye way;
    Alas, that may be seene by mee!"

"If you will not come your selfe, my Lord,
    Youle lett your chamberlaine goe with mee,
Three words that I may to him speake,
    And soone he shall come againe to thee."   80

When James Swynard came that Lady before,
    Shee let him see thorrow the weme of her ring
How many there was of English lords
    To wayte there for his master and him.

" But who beene yonder, my good Ladye,
    That walkes soe royallye on yonder greene ? "
" Yonder is Lord Hunsden, Jamye," she saye ;
    " Alas, heele doe you both tree and teene ! "

" And who beene yonder, thou gay Ladye,
    That walkes soe royallye him beside ? "   90
" Yond is Sir William Drurye, Jamye," shee sayd,
    " And a keene captain hee is, and tryde."

" How many miles is itt, thou good Ladye,
    Betwixt yond English lord and mee ? "
" Marry, thrise fifty mile, Jamy," shee sayd,
    " And even to seale and by the sea :

" I never was on English ground,
    Nor never see itt with mine eye,
But as my witt and wisedome serves,
    And as *the* Booke it telleth mee.   100

" My mother, shee was a witch woman,
    And part of itt shee learned mee ;
Shee wold let me see out of Lough Leven
    What they dyd in London cytye."

" But who is yond, thou good Layde,
    That comes yonder with an osterne ffcae ? "
" Yonds Sir John fforster, Jamye," shee sayd ;
    " Methinkes thou sholdest better know him then I."
" Even soe I doe, my goodlye Ladye,
    And ever alas, soe woe am I !   110

He pulled his hatt over his eyes,
    And, Lord, he wept soe tenderlye !
He is gone to his master againe,
    And even to tell him the veretye.

" Now hast thou beene with Marry, Jamy," he sayd,
    " Even as thy tounge will tell to mee;
But if thou trust in any womans words,
    Thou must refraine good companye."

" It is noe words, my Lord," he sayes,
    " Yonder the men shee letts me see,   120
How many English lords there is
    Is wayting there for you and mee;

" Yonder I see the Lord Hunsden,
    And hee and you is of the third degree;
A greater enemye, indeed, my Lord,
    In England none have yee."

" And I have beene in Lough Leven
    The most part of these yeeres three :
Yett had I never noe out-rake,
    Nor good games that I cold see;   130

" And I am thus bidden to yonder shooting
    By William Douglas all trulye;
Therfore speake never a word out of thy mouth
    That thou thinkes will hinder mee."

Then he writhe the gold ring of his ffingar
    And gave itt to that Ladye gay;
Sayes, " That was a legacye left unto mee
    In Harley woods where I cold bee."

" Then ffarewell hart, and farewell hand,
    And ffarwell all good companye!   140
That woman shall never beare a sonne
    Shall know soe much of your privitye."

"Now hold thy tounge, Ladye," hee sayde,
    "And make not all this dole for mee,
For I may well drinke, but Ist never eate,
    Till againe in Lough Leven I bee."

He tooke his boate att the Lough Leven
    For to sayle now over the sea,
And he hath cast upp a silver wand,
    Saies, " Fare thou well, my good Ladye!"   150
The Ladye looked over her left sholder;
    In a dead swoone there fell shee.

"Goe backe againe, Douglas!" he sayd,
    "And I will goe in thy companye,
For sudden sicknesse yonder Lady has tane,
    And ever, alas, shee will but dye!

"If ought come to yonder Ladye but good,
    Then blamed fore that I shall bee,
Because a banished man I am,
    And driven out of my owne countrye."   160

"Come on, come on, my Lord," he sayes,
    "And lett all such talking bee;
Theres ladyes enow in Lough Leven,
    And for to cheere yonder gay Ladye."

"And you will not goe your selfe, my Lord,
    You will lett my chamberlaine goe with mee;
Wee shall now take our boate againe,
    And soone wee shall overtake thee."

"Come on, come on, my Lord," he sayes,
    "And lett now all this talking bee!   170
ffor my sister is craftye enoughe
    For to beguile thousands such as you and mee."

When they had sayled fifty myle,
    Now fifty mile upon the sea,
Hee had fforgotten a message that hee
    Shold doe in Lough Leven trulye:
Hee asked ' How ffarr it was to that shooting
    That William Douglas promised mee.'

Now faire words makes fooles faine;
    And that may be seene by thy master and thee; 180
ffor you may happen think itt soone enoughe
    When-ever you that shooting see."

Jamye pulled his hatt now over his browe;
    I wott the teares fell in his eye;
And he is to his master againe,
    And ffor to tell him the veretye:

" He sayes, ' Fayre words makes fooles faine,'
    And that may be seene by you and mee,
ffor wee may happen thinke itt soone enoughe
    When-ever wee that shooting see." 190

" Hold upp thy head, Jamye," the Erle sayd,
    And never lett thy hart fayle thee;
He did itt but to prove thee with,
    And see how thow wold take with death trulye."

When they had sayled other fifty mile,
    Other fifty mile upon the sea,
Lord Peercy called to him, himselfe,
    And sayd, " Douglas, what wilt thou doe with mee?"

" Looke that your brydle be wight, my Lord,
    That you may goe as a shipp att sea; 200
Looke that your spurres be bright and sharpe,
    That you may pricke her while sheele awaye."

" What needeth this, Douglas," he sayth,
  " That thou needest to ffloute mee?
For I was counted a horsseman good
  Before that ever I mett with thee.

" A ffalse Hector hath my horsse;
  And ever an evill death may hee dye!
And Willye Armestronge hath my spurres
  And all the geere belongs to mee."   210

When they had sayled other fifty mile,
  Other fifty mile upon the sea,
They landed low by Barwicke side;
  A deputed [lord] landed Lord Percye.

ffinis

GUYE OF GISBORNE

When shales beeene sheene, and shradds full fayre,
    And leeves both large and longe,
Itt is merrry walking in the fayre fforrest
    To heare the small birds s[o]nge.

The woodweete sang and wold not cease
    Amongst the leaves a lyne;
      *   *   *
" And it is by two wight yeomen,
    By deare God that I meane:

" Me thought they did mee beate and binde,
    And tooke my bow mee froe;   10
If I bee Robin a-live in this lande,
    Ile be wrocken on both them towe."

" Sweevens are swift, master," quoth John,
    " As the wind that blowes ore a hill;
ffor if itt be never soe lowde this night,
    To-morrow it may be still."

" Buske yee, bowne yee, my merry men all!
    ffor John shall goe with mee;
For Ile goe seeke yond wight yeomen
    In greenwood where they bee."   20

They cast on their gowne of greene;
    A shooting gone are they
Untill they came to the merry greenwood
    Where they had gladdest bee;
There were they ware of *a* wight yeoman;
    His body leaned to a tree,

A sword and a dagger he wore by his side,
    Had beene many a mans bane,
And he was cladd in his capull hyde,
    Topp, and tayle, and mayne.   30

"Stand you still, master," quoth Litle John,
    "Under this trusty tree,
And I will goe to yond wight yeoman
    To know his meaning trulye."

"A, John! by me thou setts noe store,
    And thats a ffarley thinge;
How offt send I my men beffore,
    And tarry my-selfe behinde?

"It is noe cunning a knave to ken,
    And a man but heare him speake;
And itt were not for bursting of my bowe,   40
    John, I wold thy head breake."

But often words they breeden ball;
    That parted Robin and John;
John is gone to Barnsdale,
    The gates he knowes eche one.

And when hee came to Barnesdale,
    Great heavinesse there hee hadd;
He ffound two of his own fellowes
    Were slaine both in a slade,   50

And Scarlett a ffoote flyinge was
    Over stockes and stone,
For the Sheriffe with seven score men
    Fast after him is gone.

"Yett one shoote Ile shoote," sayes Litle John;
　　"With Crist his might and mayne
Ile make yond fellow that flyes soe fast
　　To be both glad and ffaine.

John bent up a good veiwe bow,
　　And ffetteled him to shoote;　　　　　　60
The bow was made of a tender boughe,
　　And fell downe to his foote.

"Woe worth thee, wicked wood!" sayd Litle John,
　　"That ere thou grew on a tree!
ffor this day thou art my bale,
　　My boote when thou shold bee!"

This shoote it was but looselye shott,
　　The arrowe flew in vaine,
And it mett one of the Sheriffes men:
　　Good William a Trent was slaine.　　　　70

It had beene better for a William Trent
　　To hange upon a gallowe
Then for to lye in the greenwoode
　　There slaine with an arrowe.

And it is sayd, when men be mett,
　　Six can doe more then three:
And they have tane Litle John
　　And bound him ffast to a tree.

"Thou shalt be drawen by dale and downe," quoth the
　　　　Sheriffe,
　　"And hanged hye on a hill."　　　　　　80
"But thou may ffayle," quoth Litle John,
　　"If itt be Christs owne will."

255

Let us leave talking of Litle John,
    For hee is bound fast to a tree,
And talke of Guy and Robin Hood
    In they green woode where they bee;

How these two yeomen together they mett
    Under the leaves of lyne,
To see what marchandise they made
    Even at that same time.   90

"Good morrow, good fellow!" quoth Sir Guy;
    "Good morrow, good ffellow!" quoth hee;
"Methinkes by this bow thou beares in thy hand,
    A good archer thou seems to bee."

"I am wilfull of my way," quoth Sir Guye,
    "And of my morning tyde."
"Ile lead thee through the wood," quoth Robin,
    "Good ffellow, Ile be thy guide."

"I seeke an outlawe," quoth Sir Guye,
    "Men call him Robin Hood;   100
I had rather meet with him upon a day
    Then forty pounds of golde."

"If you tow mett, itt wold be seene whether were better
    Afore yee did part awaye;
Let us some other pastime find,
    Good ffellow, I thee pray.

"Let us some other masteryes make,
    And wee will walke in the woods even,
Wee may chance meet with Robin Hoode
    Att some unsett steven."   110

They cutt them downe t[wo] summer shroggs
    Which grew both under a bryar,
And sett them three score rood in twinn
    To shoote the prickes full neare.

" Leade on, good ffellow," sayd Sir Guye,
    " Lead on, I doe bidd thee."
" Nay, by my faith," quoth Robin Hood,
    " The leader thou shalt bee."

The first good shoot that Robin ledd,
    Did not shoote an inch the pricke ffroe.   120
Guy was an archer good enoughe,
    But he cold neere shoote soe.

The second shoote Sir Guy shott,
    He shott within the garlande;
But Robin Hoode shott it better then hee,
    For he clove the good pricke wande.

" Gods blessing on thy heart!" sayes Guye,
    " Goode ffellow, thy shooting is goode;
For on thy hart be as good as thy hands,
    Thou were better then Robin Hood.   130

" Tell me thy name, good ffellow," quoth Guy,
    " Under the leaves of lyne."
" Nay, by my faith," quoth good Robin,
    " Till thou have told me thine."

" I dwell by dale and downe," quoth Guye,
    " And I have done many a curst turne;
And he that calles me by my right name,
    Calles me Guye of good Gysborne."

"My dwelling is in the wood," sayes Robin;
    " By thee I set right nought;   140
My name is Robin Hood of Barnesdale,
    A ffellow thou has long sought."

He that had neither beene a kithe nor kin
    Might have seene a full fayre sight,
To see how together these yeomen went
    With blades both browne and bright;

To have seene how these yeomen together fought
    Two howers of a summers day:
Itt was neither Guy nor Robin Hood
    That ffettled them to flye away.   150

Robin was reacheles on a roote,
    And stumbled at that tyde;
And Guy was quicke and nimble with-all,
    And hitt him ore the left side.

"Ah, deere Lady!" sayd Robin Hoode,
    " Thou art both Mother and may!
I thinke it was never mans destinye
    To dye before his day."

Robin thought on our Lady deere,
    And soone leapt up againe;   160
And thus he came with an awkwarde stroke;
    Good Sir Guy hee has slayne.

He tooke Sir Guys head by the hayre,
    And sticked itt on his bowes end;
" Thou hast beene traytor all thy liffe,
    Which thing must have an ende."

Robin pulled forth an Irish kniffe,
    And nicked Sir Guy in the fface,
That hee was never on a woman borne
    Cold tell who Sir Guye was :   170

Saies, " Lye there, lye there, good Sir Guye,
    And with me be not wrothe ;
If thou have had the worse stroakes at my hand,
    Thou shalt have the better cloathe."

Robin did on his gowne of greene,
    On Sir Guye hee did it throwe ;
And hee put on that capull hyde
    That cladd him topp to toe.

" The bowe, the arrowes, and litle horne,
    A[ll] with me now Ile beare ;   180
ffor now I will goe to Barnsdale,
    To see how my men doe ffare."

Robin sett Guyes horne to his mouth ;
    A lowd blast in it he did blow.
That beheard the Sheriffe of Nottingham
    As he leaned under a lowe ;

" Hearken ! hearken ! " sayd the Sheriffe,
    " I heard noe tydings but good ;
For yonder I heare Sir Guyes horne blowe,
    ffor he hath slaine Robin Hoode :   190

" ffor yonder I heare Sir Guyes horne blow,
    Itt blowes soe well in tyde,
For yonder comes that wighty yeoman
    Cladd in his capull hyde.

"Come hither, [come hither,] thou good Sir Guy!
　　Aske of mee what thou wilt have!"
"Ile none of thy gold," sayes Robin Hood,
　　"Nor Ile none of itt have;

"But now I have slaine the master," he sayd,
　　Let me goe strike the knave;　　　　　　　200
This is all the reward I aske,
　　Nor noe other will I have."

"Thou art a madman," said the Shiriffe,
　　"Thou sholdest have had a knights ffee.
Seeing thy asking beene soe badd,
　　Well granted it shall be."

But Litle John heard his master speake,
　　Well he knew that was his steven;
"Now shall I be loset," quoth Litle John,
　　"With Christs might in heaven."　　　　　210

But Robin hee hyed him towards Litle John;
　　Hee thought hee wold loose him belive.
The Sheriffe and all his companye
　　Fast after him did drive.

"Stand abacke! stand abacke!" sayd Robin;
　　"Why draw you mee soe neere?
Itt was never the use in our countrye
　　Ones shrift another shold heere."

But Robin pulled forth an Irysh kniffe,
　　And losed John hand and ffoote,　　　　　220
And gave him Sir Guyes bow in his hand,
　　And bade it be his boote.

But John tooke Guyes bow in his hand,
    His arrowes were rawstye by the roote;
The Sherriffe saw Litle John draw a bow
    And ffettle him to shoote;

Towards his house in Nottingam
    He ffled full fast away,—
And soe did all his companye,
    Not one behind did stay,—   230

But he cold neither soe fast goe,
    Nor away soe fast r[i]nn,
But Litle John with an arrow broade
    Did cleave his heart in twinn.

ffinis

HEREFFORD AND NORFOLKE

Towe noble Dukes of great renowne
    That long had lived in ffame,
Throug ffatall envye were cast downe
    And brought to sudden bane :

The Duke of Hereford was the one,
    A prudent prince and wise,
Gainst whom such mallice there was showen,
    Which soone in fight did rise.

The Duke of Norfolke most untrue
    Declared to the King,   10
' The Duke of Hereford greatly grew
    In hatred of eche thinge

Which by his Grace was acted still
    Against both hye and lowe,
And how he had a traiterous will
    His state to overthrowe.'

The Duke of Hereford then in hast
    Was sent for to the Kinge,
And by his lords in order placet
    Examined in eche thinge ;   20

Which being guiltelesse of that crime
    Which was against him layd,
The Duke of Norfolke at that time
    These words unto him sayd :

" How canst thou with a shamelesse face
    Deny a truth soe stout,
And there before his royall Grace
    Soe falselye faced itt out ?

" Did not these treasons from thee passe
    When wee together were,   30
How that the King unworthye was
    The royall crowne to weare?

" Wherfore, my gracyous lords," quoth hee,
    " And you, his noble peeres,
To whom I wish long liffe to bee,
    With many happy yeeres,

" I doe pronounce, before you all,
    The Duke of Hereford here
A traytour to our noble Kinge,
    As time shall show itt clere."   40

The Duke of Herefford hearing that,
    In mind was greeved much,
And did returne this answer fflatt,
    Which did Duke Norfolke tuche;

" The terme of traytor, trothelesse Duke,
    In scorne and deepe disdaine,
With fflatt deffyance to thy face
    I doe returne againe!

" And therfore, if it please your Grace
    To grant me grace," quoth hee,   50
" To combatt with my knowen ffoe
    That hath accused mee,

" I doe not doubt but plainlye prove,
    That like a perjured knight
Hee hath most falslye sought my shame
    Against all truth and right."

The King did grant their just request,
    And did therto agree,
Att Coventry in August next
    This combatt fought shold bee.   60

The Dukes in barbed steeds full stout,
    In coates of steele most bright,
With speares in rest did enter list,
    The combatt feirce to ffight.

The King then cast his warder downe,
    Commanding them to stay;
And with his lords some councell tooke
    To stint that mortall ffraye.

Att lenght unto the noble Dukes
    The king of heralds came,   70
And unto them with loftye speech
    This sentence did proclaime:

" With Henery Bullenbrooke this day,
    The Duke of Hereford here,
And Thomas Mawbray, Norfolkes Duke,
    Soe valyant did apeare,

" And have in honourable sorte
    Repayred to this place;
Our noble King for specyall cause
    Hath altered thus the case: 80

" ffirst, Henery Duke of Hereford,
    Ere fifteen dayes were past
Shall part this realme, on payne of death,
    While ten yeeres space doth last.

" And Thomas, Duke of Norfolke, thou
        That hast begun this striffe,—
And therfore noe good prove can bring,
        I say,—for terme of liffe,

" By judgment of our soverraine Lord
        Which now in place doth stand,
For evermore I banish thee
        Out off thy native land,

" Charging thee on payne of death,
        When fifteen dayes are past,
Thou never treade on English ground
        Soe long as liffe doth last."

Thus were they sworne before the King
        Ere they did further passe,
The one shold never come in place
        Wheras the other was.

Then both the Dukes with heaivy hart
        Were parted presentlye,
The uncoth streames of froward chance
        In forraine lands to trye.

The Duke of Norfolke cominge then
        Where *he* shold shipping take,
The bitter teares fell from his cheekes,
        And thus his moane did make :

" Now let me sob and sigh my fill
        Ere I from hence depart,
That inward panges with speed may burst
        My sore afflicted hart !

90

100

110

" Accursed man, whose lothed liffe
    Is held soe much in scorne,
Whose companye is cleane despised,
    And left as one forlorne,

" Now take thy leave and last adew
    Of this thy country deare,
Which never more thou must behold,
    Nor yett approache itt neere !   120

" How happy shold I count my selfe,
    If death my hart had torne,
That I might have my bones entombed
    Where I was bredd and borne ;

" Or that by Neptunes rathfull rage,
    I might be prest to dye,
While that sweet Englands pleasant bankes
    Did stand before mine eye.

" How sweete a sent hath Englands ground
    Within my sences now !   130
How fayre unto my outward sight
    Seemes everye branch and bowe !

" The ffeeleds, the flowers, the trees and stones,
    Seeme such unto my minde,
That in all other countreys sure,
    The like I shall not ffinde.

" Oh that the sun his shining face
    Wold stay his steeds by strenght !
That this same day might streched bee
    To twenty yeeres of lenght ;   140

" And that they true performed tyde
    Their hasty course wold stay,
That Æolus wold never yeeld
    To bring me hence away!

" That by the fountaine of mine eyes
    The ffeldes might wattered bee,
That I might grave my greevous plaints
    Upon eche springing tree!

" But time, I see, with egles wings,
    I see, doth flee away,   150
And dusty clouds begin to dimm
    The brightnesse of the day;

" The ffatall hower draweth on,
    The winds and tydes agree;
And now, sweet England, over soone
    I must depart from thee!

" The mariners have hoysed sayle,
    And call to catch me in,
And in *my* woefull hart doe feele
    My torments to begin.   160

" Wherfore, farwell for evermore,
    Sweet England, unto thee!
And farewell all my freinds, which I
    Againe shall never see!

" And England, heere I kisse th[y] ground
    Upon my bended knee,
Herby to shew to all they world
    How deere I loved thee."

This being sayd, away he went
    As fortune did him guide;   170
And att the lenght, with greefe of hart,
    In Venis there he dyed.

The other Duke in dolefull sort
    Did lead his liffe in ffrance,
And at the last the mightye Lord
    Did him ffull hiye advance.

The lords of England afterwards
    Did send for him againe,
While that King Richard in the warres
    In Ireland did remaine;   180

Who thro the vile and great abuse
    Which through his deeds did springe,
Deposed was, and then the Duke
    Was truly crowned Kinge.

ffinis

LADYES FFALL

Marke well my heavy dolefull tale,
    You loyall lovers all,
And heedfully beare in your brest
    A gallant Ladyes fall.

Long was shee wooed ere shee was woone
    To lead a wedded liffe,
But folly rought her overthrowe
    Before shee was a wiffe;

To soone, alas! she gave consent,
    And yeeleded to his will,
Tho he protested to be true
    And faithfull to her still.

Shee felt her body altered quite,
    Her bright hue waxed pale,
Her faire red cheekes changed color quite,
    Her strenght began to fayle.

And soe with many a sorrowffull sighe,
    This bewtious Ladye milde
With greeved hart perceived her selfe
    To be conceived with chyld.

Shee kept it from her parents sight
    As close as close might bee,
And soe put on her silken gowne
    None shold her swelling see.

Unto her lover secretly
   Her greefe shee did bewray,
And walking with him, hand in hand,
   These words to him did say :

" Behold," quoth shee, " a Ladyes distresse
   By love brought to your bowe ;   30
See how I goe with chyld with thee,
   Tho none thereof doth knowe !

" My litle babe springs in my wombe
   To heare it fathers voyce ;
O lett itt not be a bastard called,
   Sith I make thee my choyce !

" Thinke on thy former promises,
   Thy words and vowes eche one !
Remember with what bitter teares
   To mee thou madest thy moane !   40

" Convay me to some secrett place,
   And marry me with speede,
Or with thy rapyer end my liffe,
   Lest further shame proceede ! "

" Alacke, my derest love ! " quoth hee,
   " My greatest joy on earthe !
Which way shold I convay you hence
   To scape a sudden death !

" Your freinds are all of hye degree,
   And I of meane estate ;   50
ffull hard itt is to gett you forthe
   Out of your ffathers gate."

"Dread not your liffe to save your fame!
    For if you taken bee,
My selfe will step betweene the sword
    To take the harme of thee;

"Soe may you scape dishonor quite.
    If soe you shold be slaine,
What cold they say, but that true love
    Had wrought a Ladyes paine?   60

"But feare not any further harme;
    My selfe will soe devise,
I will safelye ryd with thee
    Unknowen of morttall eyes.

Disguised like some pretty page
    Ile meete thee in the darke,
And all alone Ile come to thee
    Hard by my ffathers parke."

"And there," quoth hee, "Ile meete my deere—
    If God doe lend me liffe—   70
On this day month without all fayle;
    Ile make thee then my wiffe."

And with a sweet and loving kisse
    They parted presentlye,
And att their partinge brinish teares
    Stoode in eche others eye.

Att lenght the wished day was come
    Wherin this lovely mayd
With longing eyes and strange attire
    For her true lover stayd.   80

If any person shee had spyed
    Came ryding ore the plaine,
Shee thought itt was her owne true love;
    But all her hopes was vaine!

Then did shee weepe, and soer bewayle
    Her most unhappy fate;
Then did shee speake these wofull words
    When succourles shee sate:

" O ffalse, fforsworne, ffaithelesse man!
    Disloyall in thy love!   90
Hast thou fforgott thy promise past,
    And wilt thou perjured proove?

" And hast thou now fforsaken mee,
    In this my greate distresse,
To end my dayes in heavinesse
    Which well thou might redresse?

" Woe worth the time I did beleeve
    That fflattering toung of thine!
Wold God that I had never seene
    The teares of thy false eyen!"   100

Soe that with many a grievous groane
    Homewards shee went amaine.
Noe rest came in her waterye eyes,
    Shee found such privy payne.

In travell strong shee fell that night
    With many a bitter thraw:—
What woefull paines shee felt that night
    Doth eche good woman knowe!—

Shee called up her waiting mayds
　　Who lay att her bedds feete,
And musing at her great woe
　　Began full fast to weepe.

"Weepe nott," shee sayth, "but shutt the dores
　　And windowes all about;
Let none bewray my wretched state,
　　But keepe all persons out!"

"O mistrus! call your mother here;
　　Of women you have neede;
And to some skilfull midwiffe helpe
　　The better may you speed."

"Call not my mother for thy liffe,
　　Nor ffeitch noe woman here!
The midwiffes helpe comes all to late;
　　My death I doe not feare."

With that the babe sprang from her wombe,
　　Noe creature being by,
And with one sighe which brake her hart
　　This gallant dame did dye.

The litle lovely infant younge,
　　The pretty smiling babe,
Resigned itt new received berath
　　To Him that had it made.

Next morning came her owne true love
　　Affrighted with this newes,
And he for sorrow slew himselfe,
　　Whom eche one did accuse.

110

120

130

2 N
　　　　273

The mother, with her new borne babe,
    Were laide both in one grave;
Their parents, overworne with woe,
    Noe joy that they cold have.   140

Take *heed* you dayntye damsells all;
    Of fflattering words beware;
And to the honor of your name
    Have you a specyall care.

ffinis

BUCKINGAM BETRAYD BY BANISTER

You barons bold, marke and behold
    The thinge that I will rite;
A story strange and yett most true
    I purpose to endite.

ffor the noble peere while he lived heere,
    The Duke of Buckingam,
He fflourisht in King Edwards time,
    The fourth king of that name.

In his service there he kept a man
    Of meane and low degree,   10
Whom he brought up then of a chyld
    From basenesse to dignitye;

He gave him lands and livings good
    Wherto he was noe heyre,
And then mached him to a gallant dame
    As rich as shee was fayre.

It came to passe in tract of time
    His wealth did soe excell,
His riches did surpasse them all
    That in that shire did dwell.   20

Who was soe brave as Banister?
    Or who durst with him contend?
Which wold not be desirous still
    To be his daylye freind?

For then it came to passe; more woe, alas!
    For sorrowes then began;
For why, the master was constraind
    To seeke succour of his man.

Then Richard the Third swaying the sword,
    Cryed himselfe a kinge,   30
Murthered two princes in their bedds,
    Which deede great striffe did bringe.

And then the Duke of Buckingam,
    Hating this bloody deede,
Against the tyrant raysed an oaste
    Of armed men indeed.

And when King Richard of this hard tell,
    A mightye ost he sent
Against the Duke of Buckingam,
    His purpose to prevent.   40

And when the Dukes people of this heard tell,
    ffeare ffilled their hearts eche one;
Many of his souldiers fledd by night,
    And left him one by one.

In extreme need the Duke tooke a steede,
    And posted night and day
Towards Banister his man,
    In secrett there to stay.

" O Banister, sweet Banister!
    Pitty thow my cause," sayes hee,   50
" And hyde me from mine enemyes
    That here accuseth mee."

" O, you be welcome, my Lord," hee sayes,
    " Your Grace is welcome here!
And as my liffe Ile keepe you safe,
    Although it cost me deere!"

" Be true, sweete Banister ! " sayes hee,
    O sweete Banister, be true ! "
" Christs curse," he sayd, " on me and mine
    If ever I prove ffalse to you ! "   60

Then the Duke cast of his velvett sute,
    His chaine of gold likwise,
And soe he did his velvett capp,
    To blind the peoples eyes;

A lethern jerkyn on his backe,
    And lethern slopps alsoe,
A heidging bill upon his backe,
    And soe into the woods did goe !

An old felt hat uppon his head,
    With twenty holes therin;   70
And soe in labor he spent the time,
    As tho some drudge he had beene.

And there he lived long unknowen,
    And still unknowne might bee,
Till Banister for hope of gaine
    Betrayd him Judaslye.

For a proclamation there was made,
    Whosoever then cold bringe
Newes of the Duke of Buckingam
    To Richard then our Kinge,   80

' A thousand markes shalbe his ffee
    Of gold and silver bright,
And then be preferred by his Grace,
    And made a worthy knight.'

And when Banister of that heard tell,
 Straight to the court sent hee,
And soe betrayd his master good
 For lucre of that ffee.

A herald of armes there was sent,
 And men with weapons good,   90
Who did attach this noble Duke
 Where he was labouring in the wood.

" Ah, ffalse Banister! a, wreched man!
 Ah, caitiffe!" then sayes hee;
" Have I maintained thy poore estate
 To deale thus Judaslye?

" Alas that ever I beleeved
 That fflattering tounge of thine!
Woe worth the time that ever I see
 That false bodye of thine!"   100

Then ffraught with feare and many a teare,
 With sorrowes almost dead,
This noble Duke of Buckingam
 Att Salsbury lost his head.

Then Banister went to the court,
 Hoping this gold to have,
But straight in prison hee was cast,
 And hard his liffe to save.

Small ffreinds he found in his distresse,
 Nor any comfort in his need,   110
But every man reviled him
 For this his trecherous deede.

And then, according to his wishe,
    Gods judgments did on him fall;
His children were consumed quite,
    His goods were wasted all;

ffor one of his sones for greeffe starke madd did fall;
    The other ffor sorrow drowned was
Within a shallow runing streame
    Where every man might passe.   120

His daugter right of bewtye bright,
    To such lewde liffe did ffall
That shee dyed in great miserye;
    And thus they were wasted all.

Old Banister lived long in shame,
    And att the lenght did dye;
And thus they Lord did plague them all
    ffor this his trecherye.

Now God blesse our King and councell grave,
    In goodness still to proceed;   130
And send every distressed man
    A better ffreind att need!

ffinis

EARLE BODWELL

Woe worth thee, woe worth thee, false Scottlande!
 ffor thou hast ever wrought by a sleight;
For the worthyest Prince, that ever was borne,
 You hanged under a cloud by night!

The Queene of ffrance a letter wrote,
 And sealed itt with hart and ringe;
And bade him come Scottland within,
 And shee wold marry him and crowne him King.

To be a King, itt is a pleasant thing;
 To bee a prince unto a peere;   10
But you have heard, and so have I too,
 A man may well by gold to deere.

There was an Italyan in that place,
 Was as welbeloved as ever was hee;
Lord David was his name,
 Chamberlaine unto the Queene was hee.

ffor if the King had risen forth of his place,
 He wold have sitt him downe in the cheare,
And tho itt beseemed him not soe well,
 Altho the King had beene present there.   20

Some lords in Scottland waxed wonderous wroth,
 And quarrelld with him for the nonce;
I shall you tell how itt beffell;
 Twelve daggers were in him all att once.

When this Queene see the chamberlaine was slaine,
 For him her cheeks shee did weete,
And made a vow for a twelve month and a day
 The King and shee wold not come in one sheete.

Then some of the lords of Scottland waxed wrothe,
 And made their vow vehementlye,   30
' For death of the Queenes chamberlaine
 The King himselfe he shall dye.'

They strowed his chamber over with gunpowder,
 And layd greene rushes in his way;
ffor the traitors thought that night
 The worthy King for to betray.

To bedd the worthy King made him bowne;
 To take his rest, that was his desire;
He was noe sooner cast on sleepe,
 But his chamber was on a blasing fyer.   40

Up he lope, and a glasse window broke;
 He had thirty foote for to ffall.
Lord Bodwell kept a privy wach
 Underneath his castle wall.
" Who have wee heere?" sayd Lord Bodwell;
 "Answer me, now I doe call."

" King Henery the Eighth my unckle was;
 Some pitty show for his sweet sake!
Ah, Lord Bodwell! I know thee well;
 Some pitty on me I pray thee take!"   50

" Ile pitty thee as much," he sayd,
 "And as much favor Ile show to thee
As thou had on the Queenes chamberlaine
 That day thou deemedst him to dye."

Through halls and towers this King they ledd,
 Through castles and towers that were hye,
Through an arbor into an orchard,
 And there hanged him in a peare tree.

When the Governor of Scottland he heard tell
 That the worthye King he was slaine,   60
He hath banished the Queene soe bitterlye
 That in Scottland shee dare not remaine;

But shee is ffled into merry England,
 And Scottland to aside hath laine;
And through the Queene of Englands good grace
 Now in England shee doth remaine.

ffinis

BISHOPPE AND BROWNE

Jesus, God! what greeffe is this
    That princes subjects cannot be true!
But still the devill and some of his
    Doth play his part, as plaine is in shew.

In Scottland dwelles a bony King
    As proper a youth as any can bee;
Hee is given to every happy thing
    That can be in a Prince to see.

On Whitsontyde, as itt befell,
    A possett was made to give the King;   10
And that his Ladye Nurse heard tell
    That itt was made a poysoned thing.
Shee cryed, and called pittiouslye,
"Helpe! or else the King must dye!

And Browne, being an Englishman,
    He did heare that Ladyes pityous crye;
But with his sword he besturred him then;
    Forth att the dore he thought to fflee,
But every dore was made full fast;
Forth of a window hee lope at last.   20

He mett the Bishopp att the dore,
    And with the possett in his hand.
The sight of Browne made the Bishopp agast;
    He bade him soe boldleye stay and stand.
With him were two that ran awaye
For feare lest Browne shold make a fray.

"Bishopp," said Browne, "What hast thou there?"
    "Nothing at all, my ffreinde," quoth hee,
"But a possett to make the King good cheere."

"Is itt soe?" sayd Browne, "that will I see;   30
Before thou goe any further inn,
Of this possett thou shalt begin."

"Browne," said the Bishopp, "I know thee well;
    Thou art a yong man both pore and bare;
And livings of thee I shall bestowe;
    Goe thou thy way, and take noe care."
"Noe!" said Browne, "that shall not bee!
Ile not be a traitor for all Christentye!
    For be itt for wayle, or for woe be itt,
    Drinke thou off this sorrowfull possett."   40

The Bishopp dranke; then by and by
    His belly burst, and he ffell downe:
A just reward for his traitorye.
    "Marry, this was a possett indeed!" said Browne.
He searched the Bishopp, and found they kayes
To goe to the King when he did please.

And when the Kinge heard tell of this,
    He meekelye fell downe on his knee,
And thanked God that he did misse
    Then of this false trecherye;   50
And then he did perceive and know
That his clergye wold have him betraid so.

He called the Nursse befor his Grace,
    And gave unto her twentye pounds a yeere.
Doughtye Browne, i' the like case,
    He dubbd him knight with gallant cheere;
Bestowed upon him livings great
For dooing such a manly feat.

ffinis

284

CHILDE WATERS

Childe Watters in his stable stoode,
    And stroaket his milke white steede :
To him came a ffaire young Ladye
    As ere did weare womans weede ;

Saies, " Christ you save, good Chyld Waters ! "
    Sayes, " Christ you save and see !
My girdle of gold which was too longe
    Is now to short ffor mee ;

" And all is with one chyld of yours,
    I ffeele sturre att my side.   10
My gowne of greene, it is to strayght ;
    Before it was to wide."

" If the child be mine, faire Ellen," he sayd,
    " Be mine, as you tell mee,
Take you Cheshire and Lancashire both,
    Take them your owne to bee.

" If the child be mine, ffaire Ellen," he said,
    " Be mine, as you doe sweare,
Take you Cheshire and Lancashire both,
    And make that child your heyre."   20

Shee saies, " I had rather have one kisse,
    Child Waters, of thy mouth,
Then I wold have Cheshire and Lancashire both,
    That lyes by north and south.

" And I had rather have a twinkling,
　　Child Waters, of your eye,
Then I wold have Cheshire and Lancashire both,
　　To take them mine oune to bee ! "

" To-morrow, Ellen, I must forth ryde
　　Soe ffarr into the north countrye ;　　　30
The ffairest Lady that I can ffind,
　　Ellen, must goe with mee."
" And ever I pray you, Child Watters,
　　Your ffootpage let me bee ! "

" If you will my ffootpage be, Ellen,
　　As you doe tell itt mee,
Then you must cutt your gownne of greene
　　An inche above your knee ;

" Soe must you doe your yellow lockes,
　　Another inch above your eye ;　　　40
You must tell noe man what is my name ;
　　My ffootpage then you shall bee."

All this long day Child Waters rode,
　　Shee ran bare ffoote by his side ;
Yett was he never soe curteous a knight,
　　To say, " Ellen, will you ryde ? "

But all this day Child Waters rode,
　　Shee ran barffoote thorow the broome !
Yett he was never soe curteous a knight
　　As to say, " Put on your shoone."　　　50

" Ride softlye," shee said, " Child Watters ;
　　Why doe you ryde soe ffast ?
The child, which is no mans but yours,
　　My bodye itt will b[ra]st."

286

He sayes, " Sees thou yonder water, Ellen,
    That fflowes from banke to brim ? "
" I trust to God, Child Waters," shee said,
    " You will never see mee swime."

But when shee came to the waters side,
    Shee sayled to the chinne :   60
" Except the Lord of heaven be my speed,
    Now must I learne to swime."

The salt waters bare up Ellens clothes ;
    Our Ladye bare upp her chinne ;
And Child Waters was a woe man, good Lord,
    To ssee faire Ellen swime.

And when shee over the water was,
    Shee then came to his knee :
He said, " Come hither, ffaire Ellen,
    Loe yonder what I see !   70

" Seest thou not yonder hall, Ellen ?
    Of redd gold shine the yates ;
Theres twenty-four ffayre ladyes,
    The ffairest is my wordlye make.

" Seest thou not yonder hall, Ellen ?
    Of redd gold shineth the tower ;
There is twenty-four ffaire ladyes,
    The fairest is my paramoure."

" I doe see the hall now, Child Waters,
    That of redd gold shineth the yates.   80
God give good then of your selfe,
    And of your wordlye make !

" I doe see the hall now, Child Waters,
    That of redd gold shineth the tower.
God give good then of your selfe
    And of your paramoure ! "

There were twenty-four ladyes,
    Were playing at the ball ;
And Ellen was the ffairest ladye,
    Must bring his steed to the stall.   90

There were twenty-four faire ladyes
    Was playing att the chesse ;
And Ellen shee was the ffairest ladye,
    Must bring his horsse to grasse.

And then bespake Child Waters sister,
    And these were the words said shee ;
" You have the prettyest ffootpage, brother,
    That ever I saw with mine eye,

" But that his belly it is soe bigg,
    His girdle goes wonderous hye ;   100
And ever I pray you, Child Waters,
    Let him goe into the chamber with mee."

" It is more meete for a litle ffootpage
    That has run through mosse and mire,
To take his supper upon his knee
    And sitt downe by the kitchin fyer,
Then to goe into the chamber with any ladye
    That weares soe *rich* attyre."

But when they had supped every one,
    To bedd they tooke they way ;   110
He sayd, " Come hither, my litle footpage,
    Hearken what I doe say !

" And goe thy downe into yonder towne,
    And low into the street;
The ffarest ladye that thou can find,
    Hyer her in mine armes to sleepe,
And take her up in thine armes two
    For filinge of her ffeete."

Ellen is gone into the towne,
    And low into the streete :
The fairest ladye that shee cold find,
    Shee hyred in his armes to sleepe,
And tooke her in her armes two
    For filing of her ffeete.

" I pray you now, good Child Waters,
    That I may creepe in att your bedds feete ;
For there is noe place about this house
    Where I may say a sleepe."

This, and itt drove now affterward
    Till itt was neere the day :
He sayd, " Rise up, my litle ffoote page,
    And give my steed corne and hay ;
And soe doe thou the good blacke oates,
    That he may carry me the better away."

And up then rose ffaire Ellen,
    And gave his steed corne and hay,
And soe shee did on the good blacke oates,
    That he might carry him the better away.

Shee layned her backe to the manger side,
    And greivouslye did groane ;
And that beheard his mother deere,
    And heard her make her moane.

Shee said, " Rise up, thou Child Waters!
    I thinke thou art a cursed man ;
For yonder is a ghost in thy stable
    That greivouslye doth groane,
Or else some woman laboures of child,
    Shee is soe woe begone ! "

But up then rose Child Waters,
    And did on his shirt of silke ;   150
Then he put on his other clothes
    On his body as white as milke.

And when he came to the stable dore,
    Full still that hee did stand,
That hee might heare now faire Ellen,
    How shee made her monand :

Shee said, " Lullabye, my owne deere child !
    Lullabye, deere child, deere !
I wold thy father were a king,
    Thy mother layd on a beere !   160

" Peace now," he said, " good faire Ellen !
    And be of good cheere, I thee pray ;
And the bridall, and the churching both,
    They shall bee upon one day."

ffinis

BESSIE OFF BEDNALL

Itt was a blind beggar that long lost his sight,
He had a faire daughter both pleasant and bright,
And many a gallant brave sutor had shee,
For none was soe comelye as pretty Bessye.

And tho shee was of ffavor most faire,
Yett seeing shee was but a beggars heyre,
Of ancyent houskeepers despised was shee,
Whose sonnes came as sutors to prettye Bessye.

Wherefore in great sorrow faire Bessy did say,
" Good ffather and mother, let me goe away   10
To seeke out my fortune, where ever itt be."
This sute then they granted to pretty Bessye.

Then Bessye, that was of bewtye soe bright,
They cladd in gray russett, and late in the night
With teares shee lamented her destinye;
Soe sadd and soe heavy was pretty Bessye.

Shee went till shee came to Stratford the Bow,
Then knew shee not whither nor which way to goe;
ffrom ffather and mother alone parted shee,
Who sighed and sobbed for pretty Bessye.   20

Shee kept on her journey till it was day,
And went unto Rumford along the hye way,
And att the Queenes Armes entertained was shee,
Soe faire and welfavoured was pretty Bessye.

Shee had not beene there a month to an end,
But master, and mistress, and all, were her ffreind;
And every brave gallant that once did her see,
Was straight-way in love with pretty Bessye.

Great guifts they did give her of silver and gold,
And in their songs daylye her love was extold;   30
Her beawtye was blessed in every degree,
Soe faire and soe comlye was pretty Bessye.

The young men of Rumford in her had their joy,
Shee showed herseffe curteous, and never to coye;
And att her commandement wold they *ever* bee,
Soe ffayre and soe comly was pretty Bessye.

ffowre sutors att once they unto her did goe,
They craved her ffavor, but still shee sayd noe;
" I wold not wish gentlemen marry with mee : "
Yett ever they honored pretty Bessye.   40

A merchant of London, whose wealth was not small,
Was there the ffirst sutor and proper with-all;
The second a genteleman of good degree,
Who wooed and sued ffor pretty Bessye;

The third of them was a gallant young knight,
And he came unto her disguised in the night;
Her mistress owne sonne the fourth man must bee,
Who swore he wold dye ffor pretty Bessye.

" And if thou wilt wedd with me," quoth the knight,
" Ile make thee a ladye with joy *and* delight;   50
My hart is inthralled by thy bewtye!
Then grant me thy ffavor, my pretty Bessye ! "

The gentleman sayd, " Marry with mee;
In silke and in velvett my Bessye shalbee;
My hart lyes distressed; O helpe me!" quoth hee,
" And grant me thy love, thou pretty Bessye!"

" Let me bee thy husband!" the merchant cold say,
" Thou shalt live in London both gallant and gay;
My shippes shall bring home rych jewells for thee;
And I will ffor ever love pretty Bessye."   60

Then Bessye shee sighed, and thus shee did say,
" My ffather and mother I meane to obey;
ffirst gett their good will, and be ffaithfull to me,
And you shall enjoye your prettye Bessye."

To every one this answer shee made,
Wherfore unto her they joyffullye sayd,
" This thing to ffulfill wee doe all agree;
And where dwells thy ffather, my pretty Bessy?"

" My ffather," shee said, " is soone to be seene;
He is the blind beggar of Bednall Greene,   70
That daylye sitts begging ffor charitye;
He is the good ffather of pretty Bessye;

" His markes and his tokens are knowen ffull well,
He alwayes is led with a dogg and a bell;
A silly blind man, God knoweth, is hee,
Yett hee is the good ffather of pretty Bessye."

" Nay, then," quoth the merchant, " thou art not for
    mee!"
" Nor," quoth the inholder, "my wiffe thou shalt bee!"
" I lothe," sayd the gentleman, " a beggars degree;
Therffore, ffarwell, my pretty Bessye!"   80

"Why then," quoth the knight, "hap better or worsse,
I way not true love by the waight of my pursse,
And bewtye is bewtye in every degree,
Then welcome to me, my pretty Bessye!

"With thee to thy ffather fforth will I goe."
"Nay sofft," quoth his kinsman, "itt must not be soe;
A beggars daughter noe ladye shalbe;
Therfore take thy due *leave* of pretty Bessye."

But soone after this, by breake of the day,
The knight ffrom Rumfford stole Bessye awaye.   90
The younge men of Rumfford, as thicke as might bee,
Rode affter to ffeitch againe pretty Bessye;

As swift as they winde to ryd they were seene
Untill they came to Bednall Greene;
And as the knight lighted most curteouslye,
They ffought against him for pretty Bessye;

But rescew speedilye came on the plaine,
Or else the young knight ffor his love had beene slaine.
This ffray being ended, then straight he did see
His kinsman came rayling against pretty Bessye.   100

Then spake the blind beggar, "Althoe I be poore,
Yett rayle not against my child at my dore;
Thoe shee be not decked in velvett and pearle,
Yett will I dropp angells with you for my girle;

"And then if my gold may better her birthe,
And equall the gold you lay on the earth,
Then neyther rayle, nor grudge you to see
The blind beggars daughter a lady to bee.

" Butt ffirst I will heare, and have itt well knowen,
The gold that you drop shall all be your owne."   110
With that they replyed, " Contented wee bee."
" Then here is," quoth the beggar, " ffor pretty Bessye."

With that an angell he dropped on the ground,
And dropped in angells five hundred pound.
And oftentimes itt was proved most plaine,
ffor the gentlemans one the beggar dropt twayne,

Soe that the place wherin they did sitt,
With gold was covered every whitt.
The gentleman having dropped all his store,
Said, " Beggar, hold! for wee have noe more.   120

" Thou hast ffulfilled thy promise arright."
" Then marry," quoth hee, " my girle to this knight;
And heere," quoth hee, " Ile throw you downe
A hundred pounds more to buy her a gowne."

The gentleman that all this treasure had seene,
Admired the beggar of Bednall Greene,
And those that were her sutors before
Their fflesh for verry anger they tore.

Then was ffaire Bessye mached to the knight,
And made a ladye in others despite;   130
A ffairer ladye was never seene
Then the Beggars daughter of Bednall Greene.

But of their sumptuous marriage and ffeast,
And what brave lords and knights thither were prest,
The second ffitt shall sett to sight,
With marveilous pleasure and wished delight.

Second Parte

Off a blind beggars daughter most bright,
That late was betrothed unto a younge knight,
All the discourse ther-of you did see:
But now comes the wedding of pretty Bessye.   140

Within a gallant pallace most brave,
Adorned with all the cost they cold have,
This wedding was kept most sumptuously,
And all ffor the creditt of pretty Bessye.

All kind of daintyes and delicates sweete
Was brought ffor the banquett, as itt most meet,
Partridge, plover, and venison most ffree,
Against the brave wedding of pretty Bessye.

This marryage through England was spread by report,
Soe that a great number therto did resort   150
Of nobles and gentles in every degree;
And all was ffor the ffame of pretty Bessye.

To church then went this gallant younge knight;
His bride ffollowed, an angell most bright,
With troopes of ladyes, the like were never seene
As went with sweet Bessye of Bednall Greene.

This marryage being solempnized then
With musicke perfourmed by the skillfullest men,
The nobles and gentles sate downe at that tyde,
Each one beholding the beautifull bryde.   160

But after the sumptuous dinner was done,
To talke and to reason a number begunn
Of the blind beggars daughter most bright,
And what with his daughter he gave to the knight.

Then spake the nobles, " Most marveill have wee,
This jolly blind beggar wee cannott here see."
" My lord," said the bride, " my father is soe base,
He is loth by his presence these states to disgrace ;

" The prayse of a woman in questyon to bringe
Before her fface heere, were a flattering thing."   170
" Wee thinke thy ffathers basenesse," quoth they,
" Might by thy bewtye be cleane put awaye."

They had noe sooner these pleasant words spoke,
But in comes the beggar cladd in a silke cote,
A vellvett capp and a ffether had hee,
And now a musityan fforsooth hee wold bee ;

And being led in, ffor catching of harme
He had a daintye lute under his arme,
Saies, " Please you to heare any musicke of mee ?
Ile sing you *a* song of pretty Bessye."   180

With that his lute he twanged straight-way,
And there begann most sweetlye to play,
And after a lesson was played two or three :
He strayned on this song most delicatelye :

" A beggars daughter did dwell on *a* greene,
Who ffor her ffaire might be a queene ;
A blithe bonny lasse, and daintye, was shee,
And many a one called her pretty Bessye."

" Her ffather hee had noe goods nor noe lands,
But begd for a penny all day with his hands ;   190
Yett to her marriage hee gave thousands three :
And still he hath somewatt for pretty Bessye ;

"And if any one her birth doe disdaine,
Her ffather is ready with might and with maine
To proove shee is come of a noble degree;
Therfore never fflout att pretty Bessye."

With that the lords and the companye round
With harty laughter were like to sound.
Att last said the lords, "Full well wee may see,
The bride and the beggar is behouldinge to thee."   200

With that the bride all blushing did rise
With the salt water within her faire eyes:
"O pardon my ffather, grave nobles," quoth shee,
"That thorrow blind affection thus doteth on mee."

"If this be thy ffather," the nobles did say,
"Well may he be proud of this happy day;
Yett by his countenance well may wee see,
His birth and his ffortune did never agree;

"And therfor, blind man, I pray thee bewray,
And looke that the truth thou to us doe say,   210
Thy birth and thy parentage, what itt may bee,
Even for the love thou bearest to pretty Bessye."

"Then give me leave, you gen[t]ells eche one,
A song more to sing, then will I goe on;
And if that itt may not winn good report,
Then doe not give me a groat for my sport.

"When ffirst our King his ffame did advance,
And fought for his title in delicate ffrance,
In many a place many perills past hee:
Then was not borne my pretty Bessye.   220

"And then in those warres went over to fight
Many a brave duke, a lord, and a knight,
And with them younge Mountford, his courage most free :
But then was not borne my pretty Bessye.

"Att Bloyes there chanced a terrible day,
Where many brave ffrenchmen upon the ground lay ;
Amonge them lay Mountford for companye :
But then was not borne my pretty Bessye.

"But there did younge Mountford, by blow on the face,
Loose both his eyes in a very short space ;   230
And alsoe his liffe had beene gone with his sight,
Had not a younge woman come forth in the night

"Amongst the slaine men, as fancy did move,
To search and to seeke for her owne true love ;
And seeing young Mountford there gasping to bee,
Shee saved his liffe through charitye.

"And then all our vittalls, in beggars attire,
Att hands of good people wee then did require.
Att last into England, as now it is seene,
Wee came, and remained att Bednall Greene ;   240

"And thus wee have lived in ffortunes despite,
Tho poore, yett contented with humble delight ;
And in my younge yeeres, a comfort to bee,
God sent mee my daughter, pretty Bessye."

"And thus, noble lords, my song I doe end,
Hoping the same noe man doth offend ;
Full forty winters thus I have beene,
A silly blind beggar of Bednall Greene."

Now when the companye everye one
Did heare the strange tale in the song he had shown,   250
They were all amazed, as well they might bee,
Both at the blind beggar and pretty Bessye.

With that he did the fayre bride imbrace,
Saying, " Thou art come of an honourablle race ;
Thy ffather likewise of a highe degree,
And thou art well worthy a lady to bee ! "

Thus was the ffeast ended with joy and delight ;
A bridegroome *blissful* was the young knight,
Who lived in joy and felicitye
With his ffaire ladye, pretty Bessye.   260

ffinis

HUGH SPENCER

The court is kept att leeve London,
    And evermore shall be itt;
The King sent for a bold embassador,
    And Sir Hugh Spencer that he hight.

" Come hither, Spencer," saith our Kinge,
    " And come thou hither unto mee,
I must make thee an embassadour
    Betweene the King of ffrance and mee.

" Thou must comend me to the King of ffrance,
    And tell him thus and now ffrom mee,   10
' I wold know whether there shold be peace in his land,
    Or open warr kept still must bee.'

" Thoust have thy shipp at thy comande,
    Thoust neither want for gold nor ffee,
Thoust have a hundred armed men
    All att thy bidding ffor to bee."

They wind itt served, and they sayled,
    And towards ffrance thus they be gone;
They wind did bring them safe to shore,
    And safelye landed everye one.   20

The ffrenchmen lay on the castle wall
    The English souldiers to be-hold:
" You are welcome, traitors, out of England;
    The heads of you are bought and sold!"

With that spake proud Spencer,
    " My leege, soe itt may not bee!
I am sent an embassador
    ffrom our English King to yee.

" The King of England greetes you well,
    And hath sent this word by mee;   30
He wold know whether there shold be peace in your
      land,
    Or open warres kept still must bee."

" Comend me to the English Kinge,
    And tell this now ffrom mee;
There shall never peace be kept in my land
    While open warres kept there may bee."

With that came downe the Queene of ffrance,
    And an angry woman then was shee;
Saies, " Itt had beene as ffitt now for a King
    To be in his chamber with his ladye,   40
Then to be pleading with traitors out of England
    Kneeling low uppon their knee."

But then bespake him proud Spencer,
    For noe man else durst speake but hee:
" You have not wiped your mouth, madam,
    Since I heard you tell a lye."

" O hold thy tounge, Spencer!" shee said,
    " I doe not come to plead with thee;
Darest thou ryde a course of warr
    With a knight that I shall put to thee?"   50

" But ever alacke!" then Spencer sayd,
  " I thinke I have deserved Gods cursse;
ffor I have not any armour heere,
  Nor yett I have no justing horsse."

" Thy shankes," quoth shee, " beneath the knee
  Are verry small above the shinne
ffor to doe any such honourablle deeds
  As the Englishmen say thou has done.

" Thy shankes beene small above thy shoone,
  And soe they beene above thy knee;   60
Thou art to slender every way,
  Any good juster ffor to bee."

" But ever alacke," said Spencer then,
  " For one steed of the English countrye!"
With that bespake and one ffrench knight,
  " This day thoust have the choyce of three:"

The first steed he ffeiched out,
  I-wis, he was milke white.
The ffirst ffoot Spencer in stirropp sett,
  His backe did from his belly ty[t]e.   70

The second steed that he ffeitcht out,
  I-wis, that hee was verry browne;
The second ffoot Spencer in stirropp settt,
  That horsse and man and all ffell downe.

The third steed that hee ffeitched out,
  I-wis, that he was verry blacke;
The third ffoote Spencer into the stirropp sett,
  He leaped on to the geldings backe.

"But ever alacke," said Spencer then,
    "For one good steed of the English countrye! 80
Goe ffeitch me hither my old hacneye
    That I brought with me hither beyond the sea."

But when his hackney there was brought,
    Spencer a merry man there was hee;
Saies, "With the grace of God and St. George of England,
    The ffeild this day shall goe with mee!

"I have not fforgotten," Spencer sayd,
    "Since there was ffeild foughten at Walsingam,
When the horsse did heare the trumpetts sound,
    He did beare ore both horsse and man."   90

The day was sett, and togetther they mett
    With great mirth and melodye,
With minstrells playing and trumpetts soundinge,
    With drumes striking loud and hye.

The ffirst race that Spencer run,
    I-wis, hee run itt wonderous sore;
He *hit* the knight upon his brest,
    But his speare itt burst, and wold touch noe more.

"But ever alacke," said Spencer then,
    "For one staffe of the English countrye!   100
Without youle bind me three together,"
    Quoth hee, "theyle be to weake ffor mee."

With that bespake him the ffrench knight,
    Sayes, "Bind him together the whole thirtye,
For I have more strenght in my to hands
    Then is in all Spencers bodye."

" But prove att parting," Spencer sayes,
    " ffrench knight, here I tell itt thee,
For I will lay thee five to four
    The bigger man I prove to bee.   110

But the day was sett, and together they mett,
    With great mirth and melodye,
With minstrells playing and trumpetts soundinge,
    With drummes strikeing loud and hye.

The second race that Spencer run,
    I-wis, hee ridd itt in much pride,
And he hitt the knight upon the brest,
    And drave him ore his horsse beside.

But he run thorrow the ffrench campe;
    Such a race was never run beffore;   120
He killed of King Charles his men
    Att hand of thirteen or fourteen score.

But he came backe againe to the King
    And kneeled him downe upon his knee,
Saies, "A knight I have slaine, and a steed I have woone,
    The best that is in this countrye."

" But nay, by my faith," said the King,
    " Spencer, soe itt shall not bee;
Ile have that traitors head of thine
    To enter plea att my jollye."   130

But Spencer looket him once about;
    He had true bretheren left but four:
He killed ther of the Kings gard
    About two or three score.

2 R   305

"But hold thy hands," the King doth say,
    "Spencer! now I doe pray thee;
And I will goe into litle England,
    Unto that cruell Kinge with thee."

"Nay, by my ffaith," Spencer sayd,
    "My leege, for soe itt shall not bee;   140
For on you sett ffoot on English ground,
    You shall be hanged upon a tree."

"Why then, comend *me* to that English Kinge,
    And tell him thus now ffrom mee,
That there shall never be open warres kept in my land
    Whilest peace kept that there may bee."

ffinis

KINGE ADLER

Kinge Adler, as hee in his window lay,
Unto a stranger knight he did say,
" I wold my lands they were as broada
As the red rose is in my garden :
There were not that woman this day alive,
I kept to bee my wedded wiffe,
Without [s]he were as white as any milke
Or as soft as any silke,
And the royall rich wine ran downe her brest bone,
And Lord! shee were and a leath maiden."   10
" But Estmere our King· has a daughter soe younge;
God Lord! shees as soft as any silke,
And as white as any milke,
The royall rich wine runes downe her brest bone,
And Lord! shee is a leath maiden."
" But will you goe unto King Ardine,
And will that ffaire lady that shee wilbe mine? "
Hee tooke the fflood, and the winde was good,
Untill hee came unto that Kings hall.
He grett them well both great and small :   20
" Kinge Adler hath sent me hither to thee,
And wills thy ffayre daughter, shee will his bee."
He sayes, " If King Adler will my daughter winne,
Of another manner he must begin :
Ifaith he shall bring lords to the mold,
One hundred shippes of good red gold,
One hundred shippes of ladyes on the moure,
One hundred shippes of wheat boulted flower,
One hundred shippes of ladyes bright,
One hundred shippes of new dubbd knights.   30
Yett he shall doe that is more pine,
He shall take the salt sea and turne itt to red wine;

307

When hee has done all these deeds,
Then my faire daughter shalbe his;
But I have sett her on such a pinn,
King Adler shall her never winne."
He tooke the flood, and they wind was good,
And never stayd in noe stead
Untill he came to Kinge Adlers hall.
He greeted them well both great and small,   40
Saies " I have beene att yonder Kings place
To speake with his daughter fayre of face;
He sayes, if you will his daughter winne,
Of another manner you must begin:
You must bring lords to the mold,
One hundred shippes of good redd gold,
One hundred shippes of ladyes of the moure,
One hundred shippes of wheat boulted flower,
One hundred shippes of ladyes bright,
One hundred shippes of new dubdd knights;   50
And yett you must doe that is more pine,
Take the salt sea and turne it to red wine;
But he hath sett her on such a pinne
That you can her never winne."
" Some thing you must doe for mee,
I tell you all in veretye;
In ladyes *clothes* will yee mee bowne,
And bring mee to that ladyes towne,
And boaird me there one yeere or towe
Amongst those ladyes for to goe,   60
And board me there yeeres two or three:
Amongst those faire ladyes for to bee."
He tooke the fflood, and the wind was good,
And he never stayd nor stoode
Untill he came to that ladyes hall:
He greeted them well both great and small,
Sayes, " Heere I have brought a fayre ladye;
From her owne ffreinds shee is comen to bee;

I must board her a yeere or tow
Amongst your ladyes for to goe."　　　　　　　　　70
These ladyes sate all on a rowe ;
Some began to cut silke, some for to sowe ;
The Kings daughter sayes, " Your ffingars are too great,
Or else your eyes beene out of seat,—
I tell you full soone anon,—
To sowe silke or lay gold on."
But ere the twelfth moneth was come and gone
He wan the farrest ladye of everye one.
They cast the lot, and one by one,
And all the ladyes everye one　　　　　　　　　80
They cast it over two or three :
King Adler ffell with the Kings daughter to lye.
But when they were in bedd laid,
These words unto her then hee said ;
Saies, " Lady, were that man this day alive
That you wold be his wedded wiffe,
And were that man soe highlye borne
That you wold be his hend lemman ? "
" There is noe man this day alive
I kept to be his wedded wiffe,　　　　　　　　　90
Without itt were King Adler, hee,
The noblest knight in Christentye.
My father hath sett me on such a pinne,
King Adler must me never winne."
" But, ladye, how and soe betyde
King Adler were in your bed hidd ?
Wold you not call them all att a stowre,
None of the ladyes within your bower ?
Nor wold you not call them all at a call,
None of the lords in your fathers hall ?　　　　　　　　　100
Nor wold you not call them all by-deene,
Your ffather the King, nor your mother the Queene ?
But soe quickly you wold gett you bowne,
To goe with King Adler out of the towne ? "

Sais shee, " If itt wold soe betyde
King Adler were in my bed hidd,
I wold not call them all in stowre,
None of the ladyes in my bower;
Nor I wold not call them all att a call,
None of the lords in my fathers hall;   110
Nor I wold not call them all by-deene,
My ffather the King, nor my mother the Queene;
But soe quicklye I wold gett me bowne
To goe with King Adler out of the towne."
" But turne thee, ladye, hither to mee!
For I am the King that speakes to thee!"
" Alacke! King Adler! I shall catch cold,
For I can never tread on the mold,
But upon rich cloth of gold
That is five thousand fold."   120
" Peace, faire lady! youst catch noe harme,
For I will carry you under mine arme."
He tooke the fflood, and the winde was good,
And he never stinted nor stood
Untill he came to his owne hall;
He greeted them well both great and small,
God send us all to be well, and none to be woe,
Untill they wine their true love soe!

ffinis

BOY AND MANTLE

In the third day of May,
    To Carleile did come
A kind curteous Child
    That cold much of wisdome.

A kirtle and a mantle
    This Child had uppon,
With brauches and ringes,
    Full richelye bedone.

He had a sute of silke
    About his middle drawne;   10
Without he cold of curtesye,
    He thought itt much shame.

"God speed thee, King Arthur,
    Sitting att thy meate!
And the goodlye Queene Guenever!
    I canott her fforgett.

"I tell you lords in this hall,
    I hett you all heate,
Except you be the more surer
    Is you for to dread."   20

He plucked out of his potewer,
    And longer wold not dwell,
He pulled forth a pretty mantle
    Betweene two nut-shells.

"Have thou here King Arthure,
　　Have thou heere of mee;
Give itt to thy comely Queene
　　Shapen as itt is alreadye;

"Itt shall never become that wiffe
　　That hath once done amisse."　　　30
Then every knight in the Kings court
　　Began to care for his wiffe.

Forth came dame Guenever;
　　To the mantle shee her [hi]ed:
The Ladye shee was new fangle,
　　But yett shee was affrayd.

When shee had taken the mantle,
　　Shee stoode as she had beene madd:
It was from the top to the toe
　　As sheeres had itt shread.　　　40

One while was itt gaule,
　　Another while was itt greene,
Another while was itt wadded,—
　　Ill itt did her beseeme,—

Another while was it blacke
　　And bore the worst hue.
"By my troth," quoth King Arthur,
　　"I thinke thou be not true."

Shee threw downe the mantle
　　That bright was of blee.　　　50
Fast with a rudd redd
　　To her chamber can shee flee;

Shee curst the weaver and the walker
    That clothe that had wrought,
And bade a vengeance on his crowne
    That hither hath itt brought;

" I had rather be in a wood
    Under a greene tree,
Then in King Arthurs court
    Shamed for to bee."   60

Kay called forth his ladye,
    And bade her come neere;
Saies, " Madam, and thou be guiltye,
    I pray thee hold thee there."

Forth came his ladye
    Shortlye and anon;
Boldly to the mantle
    Then is shee gone.

When she had tane the mantle
    And cast it her about,   70
Then was shee bare
    All above the buttocckes.

Then every knight
    That was in the Kings court
Talked, laughed, and showted,
    Full oft att that sport.

Shee threw downe the mantle
    That bright was of blee:
ffast with a red rudd
    To her chamber can shee flee.   80

Forth came an old knight
    Pattering ore a creede,
And he proferred to this litle boy
    Twenty markes to his meede,

And all the time of the Christmasse
    Willignglye to ffeede;
For why this mantle might
    Doe his wiffe some need.

When shee had tane the mantle
    Of cloth that was made,   90
Shee had no more left on her
    But a tassell and a threed.
Then every knight in the Kings court
    Bade ' evill might shee speed.'

Shee threw downe the mantle
    That bright was of blee,
And fast with a redd rudd
    To her chamber can shee flee.

Craddocke called forth his ladye,
    And bade her come in;   100
Saith " Winne this mantle, ladye,
    With a little dinne;

" Winne this mantle, ladye,
    And it shalbe thine
If thou never did amisse
    Since thou wast mine."

Forth came Craddockes ladye
    Shortlye and anon,
But boldlye to the mantle
    Then is shee gone.   110

When shee had tane the mantle
    And cast itt her about,
Upp att her great toe
    Itt began to crinkle and crowt;
Shee sayd, " Bowe downe, mantle,
    And shame me not for nought ;

" Once I did amisse,
    I tell you certainlye,
When I kist Craddockes mouth
    Under a greene tree,   120
When I kist Craddockes mouth
    Before he marryed mee."

When shee had her shreeven,
    And her sines shee had tolde,
The mantle stoode about her
    Right as shee wold,

Seemelye of coulour,
    Glittering like gold.
Then every knight in Arthurs court
    Did her behold.   130

Then spake Dame Guenever
    To Arthur our King,
" She hath tane yonder mantle,
    Not with wright but with wronge!

" See you not yonder woman
    That maketh her selfe soe clea[n]e ?
I have seene tane out of her bedd
    Of men fiveteene,

" Preists, clarkes, and wedded men
    From her by-deene!   140
Yett shee taketh the mantle
    And maketh her-selfe cleane!"

Then spake the litle Boy
    That kept the mantle in hold;
Sayes " King! chasten thy wiffe!
    Of her words shee is to bold.

" Shee is a bitch and a witch,
    And a whore bold!
King, in thine owne hall
    Thou art a cuchold!"   150

A litle Boy stoode
    Looking over a dore;
    He was ware of a wyld bore
Wold have werryed a man.

He pulld forth a wood kniffe!
    Fast thither that he ran;
He brought in the bores head,
    And quitted him like a man.

He brought in the bores head,
    And was wonderous bold: 160
He said, " There was never a cucholds kniffe
    Carve itt that cold."

Some rubbed their knives
    Uppon a whetstone;
Some threw them under the table,
    And said they had none.

King Arthus and the Child
  Stood looking them upon;
All their knives edges
  Turned backe againe.   170

Craddoccke had a litle knive
  Of iron and of steele;
He birtled the bores head
  Wonderous weele,
That every knight in the Kings court
  Had a morssell.

The litle Boy had a horne
  Of red gold that ronge;
He said, "There was noe cuckolde
  Shall drinke of my horne,   180
But he shold itt sheede
  Either behind or beforne."

Some shedd on their shoulder,
  And some on their knee;
He that cold not hitt his mouth
  Put it in his eye;
And he that was a cuckold,
  Every man might him see.

Craddoccke wan the horne
  And the bores head;   190
His ladye wan the mantle
  Unto her meede.
Everye such a lovely ladye,
  God send her well to speede!

ffinis

WHITE ROSE AND RED

When Yorke and Lancaster made warre
    Within this ffamous land,
The lives of all our noble men
    Did in great danger stand.

Seven kings in bloodye ffeilde
    ffor Englands crowne did ffight,
And yett their heyres were, all but twaine,
    Of liffe bereaved quite.

Ther thirty thousand Englishmen
    Were in one battell slaine;   10
Yett all that English blood cold not
    One setled peace obtaine.

Fathers killed their owne deare sonne[s],
    The sonnes the ffathers slew,
And kinsmen ffought against their King,
    And none eche other knew.

Att lenght, by Heneryes lawfull claime,
    These wasting warres had end,
For Englands peace he did restore,
    And did the same defend.   20

ffor tyrant Richard named the Third,
    The breeder of this woe,
By him was slaine nere Leister towne,
    As chronicles doe shoe.

All ffeare of warr was then exiled,
    Which joyed eche Englishman;
And dayes of long desired peace
    Within this land began.

He ruled this kingdome by true love,
    To gaine his subjects lives;   30
Then men lived quietly att home
    With their children and their wives.

King Henery tooke such princely care
    Our ffurther peace to frame,
Tooke ffaire Elizabeth to wiffe,
    That gallant Yorkshire Dame.

Four Edwardes daughter, blest of God,
    To scape King Edwards spight,
Was thus made Englands peereles Queene,
    And Heneryes hartes delight.   40

This Henery, ffirst of Tuders name
    And last of Lancaster,
With Yorkes right heyre a true loves knott
    Did knitt and make ffast there.

Renowned Yorke, the white rose gave;
    Brave Lancaster the redd;
By wedlocke both in[j]oyned were
    To lye in one princely bed.

These roses grew, and buded fayre,
    And with soe good a grace,   50
That Kings of England in their armes
    Affords a worthy place.

And fflourish may these roses still,
 That all they world may tell
The owners of these princely fflowers
 In vertue to exell!

To glorifye these roses more,
 King Henerye and his Queene
Did place their pictures in red gold,
 Most gorgeous to be seene.   60

The Kings owne guard doe weare them now
 Upon their backe and brest,
Where love and loyaltye remaines,
 And evermore may rest.

The red rose on the backe is placed,
 Theron a crowne of gold;
The white rose on the brest as rich,
 And castlye to behold,

Bedecket with silver studdes,
 And coates of scarlett and redd,   70
A blushing hew, which Englands fame
 This many yeeres hath spredd.

This Tudor and Plantaginett
 These honors ffirst devised
To welcome home a settled peace
 By us soe dearlye prized:

Which peace now maintained is
 By James our gracyous Kinge;
ffor peace brings plentye to this land,
 With many a blessed thing.   80

To speake of Heneryes praise againe :
    His princley liberall hand
Gave guiffts and graces many wayes
    Unto this ffamous land.

Wherfore the Lord him blessing sent
    For to encrease his store,
For that he left more welthe to us
    Then any King before.

The ffirst blessing was to his Queene,
    A giuft above the rest,   90
Which brought him sonnes and daughters faire
    To make his kingdome blest.

The royall blood, which was att ebbe,
    Soe encreased by this Queene,
That Englands heyre unto this day
    Doth fflourish ffresh and greene.

The first blossome of this seed
    Was Arthur, Prince of Wales,
Whose vertue to the Spanish court
    Quite ore the ocean sayles,   100

Where fferdinando, King of Spayne,
    His daughter Katherine gave
ffor wiffe unto this English Prince
    A thing which God wold have.

Yett Arthur, in his loftye youth,
    And blooming time of age,
Resigned up his sweetest liffe
    To deathes imperyall rage.

Who dying thus, noe isue left,—
    The sweet of natures joy,—   110
Did compasse England round with greeffe,
    And Spaine with sadd annoye.

Yett Henery, to increase his joy,
    A Henery of his name,
In ffollowing time Eighth Henery called,
    A King of worthy ffame;

He conquered Bullein with his sword,
    And many townes of ffrance;
His kinglye manhood and his fortitude
    Did Englands ffame advance.   120

Then popish abbyes he supprest,
    And Pappistrye put downe,
And bound their land by Parlaiment
    Unto his royall crowne.

He had three children by three Queenes,
    All princes raigning here,
Edward, Marry, and Elizabeth,
    A Queene beloved most deere.

Yett these three branches bare noe fruite;
    Noe such blessing God did send;   130
Wherby the King by Tudors name
    In England here hath end.

Plantaginett ffirst Tudor was
    Named Elizabeth;
Ellizabeth last Tudor was,
    The greatest Queene on earth.

This Tudor and Plantaginett,
    By yeelding unto death,
Have made steward now the greatest King
    That is now upon the earth.   140

To speake of the Seventh Henery I must,
    Whose Grace gave ffree consent
To have his daughters marryed both
    To kings of his descent.

His eldest daughter Margarett
    Was made great Scottlands Queene,
As wise, as ffaire, as vertuous,
    As ever was ladye seene.

Of this faire Queene our royall King
    By lineall course descended,   150
Which weareth now the imperyall crowne,
    Which God now still defendeth.

His second daughter, Marye called,
    As princelye by degree,
Was by her ffather worthy thought
    The Queene of ffrance to bee;

And after to the Duke of Suffollke
    Was made a noble wiffe;
And in this ffamous English court
    Shee led a virtuous liffe.   160

Thus Henery and his lovely Queene
    Rejoced to see that day,
To have their children thus advancet
    To honors every way,

Which purchased pleasure and content
    With many a yeeres delight,
Till sad mischance by cruell death
    Procured them both a spighte.

This worthy Queene, this gracyous Dame,
    This mother meeke and mild,   170
To add more number to their joyes,
    Againe proved bigg with child;

Wheratt the King rejoced much,
    And against that carefull hower
He lodged his deere and lovelye Queene
    In Londons stately Tower.

Which Tower proved ffatall once
    To princes of degree;
Itt proved ffatall to this Queene,
    For therin died shee,   180

In child bed *she* lost her sweet liffe,
    Her liffe estemed soe deere,
Which had beene England lovely Queene
    Many a happy yeere.

Therfore the King was greeved sore,
    And many monthes did mourne,
And wept and sighet, and said 'like her
    He cold not ffind out one;

'Nor none he wold in ffancy chuse
    To make his wedded wiffe,   190
But a widdower he wold remaine
    The remnant of his liffe.'

His latter dayes he spent in peace
    And quiettnesse of mind.
Like King and Queene as these two were,
    The world can hardlye ffind!

Yett such a King as now wee have,
    And such a Queene wee had,
Who hath heavenly powers from above,
    And giu[f]ts as they two hadd.   200

God save our Prince, and King and land,
    And send them long to raigine!
In health, in welth, in quietnesse,
    Amongst us to remaine!

ffinis

BELL MY WIFFE

" This winters weather itt waxeth cold,
 And ffrost itt ffreeseth on every hill,
And Boreas blowes his blasts soe bold
 That all our cattell are like to spill.
Bell my wiffe, shee loves noe strife,
 Shee sayd unto m[e] quietlye,
' Rise up, and save cow Crumbockes liffe!
 Man! put thine old cloake about thee!'

" O Bell my wiffe! why dost thou fflyte?
 Thou kens my cloake is verry thin;   10
Itt is soe sore over worne,
 A cricke theron cannott r[i]nn:
Ile goe ffind the court within,
 Ile noe longer lend nor borrow;
Ile goe ffind the court within,
 For Ile have a new cloake about me."

" Cow Crumbocke is a very good cowe,
 Shee has alwayes beene good to the pale,
Shee has helpt us to butter and cheese, I trow,
 And other things shee will not fayle; 20
For I wold be loth to see her pine;
 Therfore, good husband, ffollow my councell now,
Forsake the court, and follow the ploughe;
 Man! take thine old coate about thee!"

" My cloake itt was a verry good cloake,
 It hath beene alwayes good to the weare,
Itt hath cost mee many a groat,
 I have had itt this forty-four yeere;

326

Sometime itt was of the cloth in graine,
  Itt is now but a sigh clout, as you may see; 30
It will neither hold out winde nor raine;
  And Ile have a new kloake about mee."

" It is forty-four yeeres agoe
  Since the one of us the other did ken,
And wee have had betwixt us both
  Children either nine or ten;
Wee have brought them up to women and men;
  In the feare of God I trowe they bee:
And why wilt thou thy selfe misken?
  Man! take thine old cloake about thee!" 40

" O Bell my wiffe! why doest thou flyte?
  Now is nowe, and then was then;
Seeke all the world now throughout,
  Thou kens not clownes from gentlemen;
They are cladd in blacke, greene, yellow, and blew,
  Soe ffarr above their owne degree;
Once in my liffe Ile take a vew,
  ffor Ile have a new cloake about mee."

" King Harry was a verry good King;
  I trow his hose cost but a crowne; 50
He thought them twelve pence over to deere,
  Therfore he called the taylor clowne.
He was King and wore the crowne,
  And thouse but of a low degree;
Itts pride that putts this cumtrye downe;
  Man! put thye old cloake about thee!"

" O Bell my wiffe! why dost thou fflyte?
  Now is now, and then was then;

327

Wee will live now obedyent liffe,
 Thou the woman, and I the man.
Itts not ffor a man with a woman to threape
 Unlesse he ffirst give over the play;
Wee will live noue as wee began,
 And Ile have mine old cloake abaut me."

ffinis

I LIVE WHERE I LOVE

With my hart my love was nes[t]ed
    Into the sonne of happynesse;
ffrom my love my liffe was rested
    Into a world of heavinesse;
O lett my love my liffe remaine,
Since I love not where I wold.

Darksome distance doth devyde us,
    ffar ffrom thee I must remaine;
Dismall planetts still doth guide us,
    ffearing wee shold meete againe;   10
But ffroward ffortune once removed,
Then will I live where I wold.

Iff I send them, doe not suspect mee;
    But if I come, then am I seene;
O let thy wisdome soe direct mee
    That I may blind Argus eyen!
For my true hart shall never remove,
    Tho I live not where I love.

Sweete! what greeffe have I sustained
    In the accomplishing my desires!   20
My affections are not ffained,
    Tho my wish be nere the nere.
If wishes would substantiall prove,
Then would I live where I love.

True conceit be still my feeding,
    And the ffood being soe conceipted,

Whilest my hart for thee lyes bleeding,
　　Sunne and heavens to be intreated;
Perhaps my orisons then may move,
That I may live where I love.　　　　　　　　　　　30

Love and ffaction still agreeing,
　　By the consent of heavens electyon,
Where wee both may have our being,
　　Underneath the heavens protectyon,
And smiling att our sorrowes past,
Wee shall enjoye our wishe att last.

ffinis

END OF SECOND VOLUME

PR
1181
F46⁵
v.2

Percy, Thomas
    Folio of Old English
ballads and romances

PLEASE DO NOT REMOVE
CARDS OR SLIPS FROM THIS POCKET

UNIVERSITY OF TORONTO LIBRARY

ImTheStory.com

Personalized Classic Books in many genre's

Unique gift for kids, partners, friends, colleagues

Customize:

- Character Names
- Upload your own front/back cover images (optional)
- Inscribe a personal message/dedication on the
  inside page (optional)

Customize many titles Including

- Alice in Wonderland
- Romeo and Juliet
- The Wizard of Oz
- A Christmas Carol
- Dracula
- Dr. Jekyll & Mr. Hyde
- And more...

Printed by BoD™in Norderstedt, Germany